The Action Research Guidebook

D0775016

**CORWIN
PRESS**

The Corwin Press logo—a raven striding across an open book—represents the union of courage and learning. Corwin Press is committed to improving education for all learners by publishing books and other professional development resources for those serving the field of K–12 education. By providing practical, hands-on materials, Corwin Press continues to carry out the promise of its motto: **"Helping Educators Do Their Work Better."**

The Action Research Guidebook

A Four-Step Process for Educators and School Teams

RICHARD SAGOR

CORWIN PRESS
A Sage Publications Company
Thousand Oaks, California

Copyright © 2005 by Corwin Press.

All rights reserved. When forms and sample documents are included, their use is authorized only by educators, local school sites, and/or noncommercial entities who have purchased the book. Except for that usage, no part of this book may be reproduced or utilized in any form or by any means, electronic or mechanical, including photocopying, recording, or by any information storage and retrieval system, without permission in writing from the publisher.

For information:

Corwin Press
A Sage Publications Company
2455 Teller Road
Thousand Oaks, California 91320
www.corwinpress.com

Sage Publications Ltd.
1 Oliver's Yard
55 City Road
London EC1Y 1SP
United Kingdom

Sage Publications India Pvt. Ltd.
B-42, Panchsheel Enclave
Post Box 4109
New Delhi 110 017 India

Printed in the United States of America

Library of Congress Cataloging-in-Publication Data

Sagor, Richard.
The action research guidebook: A four-step process for educators and school teams / Richard Sagor.
  p. cm.
Includes bibliographical references and index.
ISBN 978-0-7619-3894-1 (cloth) – ISBN 978-0-7619-3895-8 (pbk.)
  1. Action research in education. 2. Teachers—In-service training. I. Title.
LB1028.24.S33 2005
370.' 7' 2—dc22

                            2004008099

                07   10   9   8   7   6   5

Acquisitions Editor:	Rachel Livsey
Editorial Assistant:	Phyllis Cappello
Production Editor:	Melanie Birdsall
Copy Editor:	Marilyn Power Scott
Typesetter:	C&M Digitals (P) Ltd.
Proofreader:	Teresa Herlinger
Indexer:	Sheila Bodell
Cover Designer:	Michael Dubowe

Contents

Preface

Thank you for choosing education as your career. There is no better way to make a contribution to society and to our collective futures than investing in the growth and development of youth. In their book, *Good Work: Where Excellence and Ethics Meet*, Howard Gardner, Mihaly Csikzentmihalyi, and William Damon (2001) begin by defining the concept of *good work*. They view it as an endeavor that includes both meanings of the word "good": a pursuit that simultaneously results in a product or service that is good for society *and* that is done well. They then proceed to explore the specific conditions that support and occasionally detract from the ability of practitioners to do good work.

Teaching certainly fulfills the first part of the definition of good work; it is a pursuit that makes the world better. But for many teachers, the second aspect of it is hard to obtain. Too often teachers are forced to fight their way through conditions that make providing excellent instruction difficult, if not impossible. I wrote this book to contribute to changing this unfortunate state of affairs.

I believe that when and where teachers engage in the processes of action research and are well supported in their efforts, it is much easier for good work to occur. I hope you will come to believe this, too. It is my deepest hope that this book will play a role in helping you, the reader, experience the profound satisfaction that comes from the practice of this sacred calling.

More than anything, I believe that the practice of education is a thoughtful endeavor. Consequently, I have an aversion to professional development that is overly prescriptive and attempts to tell teachers precisely how they should go about doing their work. Feeling this way made me a bit anxious as I approached the task of writing this book.

It was my hope to produce a handbook that would provide the busy educator who wished to experience the action research process with an easy-to-follow template, one which could be readily adapted to a variety of professional interests and foci. I hope I succeeded in accomplishing that goal. But if that were all, I would have disappointed myself. I would have simply written one more step-by-step how-to manual. And in doing so, I would not have acknowledged the complexity of the issues educators confront on a daily basis. Because every educational context and every learner is different, excellent teaching requires constant creative problem solving by the expert in the classroom. Any book that contends to provide a one-size-fits-all prescription for the problems of the classroom teacher ignores this reality and by doing so, treats the professional reader in a condescending fashion. In writing this book, my goal was to provide you with two things:

1. Examples and step-by-step instructions for carrying out the action research process

2. A discussion of the rationale for and function of each of the components that make up the action research process

If you are new to action research, I hope the step-by-step instructions will enable you to have a productive and professionally fulfilling first-time experience with practitioner research. Furthermore, I hope the discussion of the rationale for these procedures will help you creatively incorporate each of the stages of the process into the particular context of your work and adapt them to your own priorities. Later, as you become a more experienced action researcher, you will undoubtedly choose to modify and customize many of the strategies presented here, as well as invent new ones, as you use the four stages of the action research process to achieve your own professional goals.

If you are already an experienced action researcher, I encourage you to look at the activities provided in this book as illustrative suggestions from a fellow educator. Use this book as a potpourri of ideas, which you might choose to try out as written, or use to stimulate alternative creative approaches that support your search for answers to the perplexing questions of practice that you are currently struggling with.

As a handbook, this text was written to be used *while* you are working your way through the action research process. I don't recommend that you sit down and read through the entire book at once. Rather, I envision you reading through a section as you are preparing to work through that stage of your action research project. The intent of each chapter is to provide concrete strategies for immediate use. Consequently, the book has been organized sequentially, and each activity as well as each discussion is conceptually built on what has gone before.

If you are using the handbook in this way—as a personal guidebook to provide guidance as you work your way through an action research project—it likely means that there may be several days, weeks, or sometimes even months between the reading of chapters. For this reason, most chapters start with a brief review of previous material to provide continuity.

One of the wonderful things about the action research process is that it is relevant to all professionals, not just educators, who wish to improve their practices. This book, however, was written for an audience of practicing K–12 educators. Even so, readers are likely to have diverse responsibilities. Some are primarily working in classrooms, while others may be administrators or specialists. My goal was to write a book that would be useful for any K–12 educator who was interested in conducting action research. This presented me with a dilemma. I could have written a book without specific examples and discussed each aspect of the action research process in general terms. But being a concrete learner myself, I understand things best when I am offered specific examples of what ideas look like in practice. Unfortunately, space limitations made it impracticable to include illustrations drawn from the full range of issues confronting the diverse practitioners of K–12 education. I resolved this by attempting to provide a little bit of everything.

Each activity and every discussion is accompanied by illustrative examples. In the pages that follow, you will meet a teacher attempting to improve student reading skills, a fifth-grade teacher struggling with an ADHD student, a principal trying to transform a school into a more collegial workplace, and a middle school language arts teacher attempting to improve students' ability to write a five-paragraph persuasive essay. You will also meet school faculties that are working collaboratively on campuswide issues. In each of these examples, the researchers use the same four-stage process; however, you will see them using it in a manner that fits their particular priorities. Each example has been drawn from the work of real educators who I've had the pleasure of working with or have observed while they conducted their action research projects. I have turned these folks into hypothetical examples by liberally combining bits and pieces of different projects to better illustrate a concept. Due to the diversity of the examples, you may need to provide your own simultaneous translation. For example, when you read something like, "When the *students* you are working with . . . ," feel free to substitute "parents," "teachers," "counselees," or "team members,"—whichever fits your context best.

As you proceed through the book, you will see that while action research can be undertaken by everyone—teachers, administrators, counselors, and specialists, from people with building responsibilities to those with district duties—their fundamental rationales for doing so may differ.

There are two principal categories of action research: *descriptive research,* studies whose purpose is to illuminate what is occurring in a particular setting; and *quasi-experimental research,* inquiries designed to test a hypothesis or a chosen innovation being implemented by the practitioner. This is another case where my goal as the author was to be inclusive. I wanted to address both types of action research, but due to space limitations, it wasn't possible to illustrate every single concept with multiple examples.

Considering all the pressure today's teachers face, it would be nice if they could call a time-out in order to get definitive answers to perplexing problems. But, since that isn't possible, they are frequently obliged to simply go with what seems best. As a result, when most educators first engage in action research, their goal is to determine if the actions they have decided to take (their hypotheses) are working as they had hoped, which explains why most action research is quasi-experimental.

Therefore I will introduce each topic in terms of how it applies to quasi-experimental research and then follow with examples of how it can be used with descriptive research, if the process is different.

What originally attracted me to action research was how well it serves the needs of the reflective professional. I define *professional* this way: Someone capable of combining a mastery of the professional knowledge base along with the wisdom of practice to creatively solve *nonroutine problems* as they arise.

Clearly, it doesn't take a professional to solve a routine problem. Anyone who can follow a recipe is able to do that. But it is the nonroutine problem, the issue that doesn't respond as the textbook says it should, that requires the application of creative problem solving.

Since no two classrooms, students, schools, or faculty ever respond the same way, every context in education is, in fact, nonroutine. Every day, there is another unique puzzle to solve. And that's why conducting action research in our own context is so critical. It is through the development of contextually sensitive insights that we can build the wisdom of practice that is so critical for excellence in professional practice.

Every day the classroom provides a learning experience for us as well as the students. Inevitably, you emerge wiser than the day before as a result of your reflective practice.

Hopefully, conducting action research will help you better understand the efficacy of your practice as you document the impact of your work on the variety of learners with whom you work. Every day, you receive feedback through the dynamic relationship of teacher and learner, and that feedback fuels growth.

I, too, have a need to grow professionally and would very much appreciate your feedback on the effectiveness of this handbook. As I wrote it, I imagined myself interacting with each of you. So, as you explore the ideas in this book, I would love to know about your experiences. Please write and share your ideas, your experience, and your wisdom.

In closing, I want to extend to each of you my very best wishes. I hope you find action research to be as enriching as I have. I hope this book proves helpful as you explore and enrich your work and endeavor to enrich the lives of those you work with. But most of all, I hope your work provides you every ounce of joy, fulfillment, and satisfaction that is humanly possible. As you do your "good work," empowering the young, you enrich us all.

About the Author

Richard Sagor founded ISIE (pronounced "I see"), the Institute for the Study of Inquiry in Education, in 1997, to work with schools and educational organizations on the use of action research and data-based school improvement while he was a professor of educational leadership at Washington State University (WSU).

Prior to joining the faculty at WSU, Sagor had 14 years of public school administrative experience, including service as an assistant superintendent, high school principal, instruction vice principal, disciplinary vice principal, and alternative school head teacher. He has taught the entire range of students, from the gifted to the learning disabled, in the areas of social studies, reading, and written composition.

Educated in the public schools of New York, Sagor received his BA from New York University and two MA degrees as well as a PhD in Curriculum and Instruction from the University of Oregon.

Beyond his work as a teacher and administrator, Sagor has had extensive international consulting experience. He served as a site visitor for the United States Department of Education's Secondary School Recognition Program and has worked with the Department of Defense's overseas schools, numerous state departments of education, and over 200 separate school districts across North America. His consulting has focused primarily on leadership development, the use of data with standards-based school improvement, collaborative action research, teacher motivation, and teaching at-risk youth.

His articles on school reform and action research have received awards from the National Association of Secondary School Principals and the Educational Press Association of America. Sagor's books include *The TQE Principal: A Transformed Leader; At-Risk Students: Reaching and Teaching Them; How To Conduct Collaborative Action Research; Local Control and Accountability: Getting it, Keeping it, and Improving School Performance; Guiding School Improvement With Action Research,* and *Motivating Students and Teachers in an Era of Standards.*

Sagor can be contacted at the Institute for the Study of Inquiry in Education, 16420 SE McGillivray, Suite 103–239, Vancouver, WA 98683, or by e-mail at rdsagor@ isie.org.

1

Introduction to Action Research

Action research: "A disciplined process of inquiry conducted by and for those taking the action. The primary reason for engaging in action research is to assist the actor in improving or refining his or her actions."

—Sagor (2000)

WHY CONDUCT ACTION RESEARCH? ■

Listening to the media, one could easily conclude that those most passionate about school improvement are the consumers of education, parents, students, and their future employers. But while the general public is clearly interested in school reform, no group of people is more passionate about promoting universal student success than classroom teachers. Most days, even the most celebrated teachers teaching highly successful students leave their classrooms frustrated, feeling that despite their best efforts, they failed to help every student progress as far as he or she might. The ritual is replayed on a daily basis; the exhausted teachers drive home wondering why things hadn't gone better and then hoping against hope that tomorrow would be a better day.

I doubt that there's a single teacher working today who didn't enter the profession committed to helping every single student prosper. Andy Hargreaves (1991) has pointed out that the greatest emotional battle teachers face today is guilt. This is borne of the realization that they aren't generating the levels of success they had desperately wanted and still hope to achieve. Anyone who has engaged in the art and science of teaching knows that this debilitating experience of continually falling short of your own high expectations is not the result of a lack of commitment, caring, or intellect. So what does account for this situation?

Several things conspire to keep teachers in this chronic state of falling short. One is the high expectations that teachers, parents, and society set. There is no question that the higher the bar, the greater the pressure. But no one who cares about youth would want to set the bar lower. Nevertheless, it must be acknowledged that the goal of universal student success, a dream held by most teachers and an expectation now codified in state and federal regulations, has never been achieved on a large scale. To my knowledge, in the history of humankind, no community has ever succeeded in getting *all* its children to high levels of performance on meaningful standards—which is the current expectation of education policy throughout North America. Therefore, not only are today's teachers in pursuit of high expectations, but they are also being pushed to travel where no one has traveled before. And they are going into this wilderness without a guidebook, a map, or a recipe.

Besides having to meet their own and society's high expectations, there are two other significant factors that contribute to chronic teacher frustration:

- The complexity of the art and science of teaching
- The way teacher work is organized

The good news is that both of these can be addressed without having to abandon the high expectations we hold for our students.

■ THE COMPLEXITY OF TEACHING

Any problem, be it personal, social, or scientific, can be expressed in the form of a mathematical equation. Arriving at a solution requires giving consideration to all potential possibilities and probabilities. Every variable (factor) involved in the decision needs to be considered in light of (multiplied by) each of the other variables. For example, when I am deciding what I should wear to work on Thursday, the decision-making equation that expresses this problem is

$$(A) \times (B) \times (C) \times (D) = X$$

A = Shirt choices

B = Pants choices

C = Tie choices

D = Shoe choices

The problem confronted at least 12 times per day by the elementary teacher and minimally 5 times daily by the secondary teacher is determining the best answer to this question:

What is the most appropriate strategy for teaching this material to this particular group of learners?

Coming up with a solution requires the teacher to consider a multitude of variables. To illustrate, let's assume I am a middle school math teacher who is preparing to introduce the concept of signed numbers. The variables that I must take into account begin with all the relevant affective factors. For example, I will need to consider how each one of my students feels about me, about math, about themselves as math learners, about our classroom, and so forth. Then I will need to multiply these variables by 30, if that's the number of students I've been assigned and assuming my goal is to meet the needs of each of them. If this looks complex, just wait; this is only the beginning.

Of course, I must also take into account the cognitive characteristics of each learner. For example, what prerequisite skills do the students possess or what skills are students missing? Where they are developmentally? What is their strongest learning style? And what conceptual understandings are they bringing to this particular math concept?

That's a lot to take into account, but simply knowing the affective and cognitive characteristics of my students is only one aspect of the equation. Even if I know each student perfectly, that still doesn't tell me how to teach them. There are at least two other things I must consider when designing my lesson. As a professional, I will want to apply everything I know about pedagogy (methods of teaching). For example, I could elect to teach this bit of content using direct instruction. Or I could use individually guided instruction, cooperative learning, modeling, and so on. As complex as all this is, just considering these factors isn't enough. For deep learning to occur, my lesson plan should also be grounded in a thorough understanding of the discipline itself. Specifically, what is the rationale for teaching this particular piece of content (in this case, signed numbers)? How does this fit conceptually with previous content and upcoming material? What are the specific skills I will want my students to gain from the study of this material?

Without belaboring the statistical aspect of this decision-making equation, it should now be clear that each and every lesson-planning decision made by a professional teacher requires the consideration and integration of literally thousands of factors. In reality, designing appropriate lessons for public school students is one of the most complex tasks any contemporary professional ever has to face.

But the complexity of the decision making is only part of the problem. After all, in many fields, being expected to creatively solve complex problems is not a source of dissatisfaction. In fact for many professionals, engaging in problem solving is what makes the work fun and motivating. Even as complex as teaching is, we aren't the only practitioners that are expected to grapple with perplexing, mind-numbing problems on a daily basis. So why does the complexity of the work create more frustration for educators than for most other professionals?

To answer that question, we need to take a look at the second problematic issue: the work context for most teachers. Even if the issues that a professional must overcome are complex, when the working conditions are such that the practitioner has reason to believe there is a decent chance of prevailing, there is justification for optimism. Unfortunately, the reverse is also true: If the conditions of work are such that it is unreasonable for a person to expect success, then pessimism, alienation, and burnout should be expected.

In other fields where practitioners are expected to prevail over unique and complex problems, two types of support are usually present: planning time and support staff. Unfortunately, neither adequate planning time nor support staff is being provided for today's teachers. These are critical working conditions that ought to be addressed, and hopefully, we will one day secure the political will necessary to provide these resources for teachers. Realistically, however, this isn't likely to occur in the near future. On the positive side, there are other things we can do to address the conditions of work in the short run. This is where this book fits in.

Action research is a small idea. Although there isn't one universally accepted set of processes that constitutes action research, as presented here, it is a simple four-stage process:

1. Clarifying vision and targets

2. Articulating theory

3. Implementing action and collecting data

4. Reflecting on data and planning informed action

These four stages help us bring to the surface the critical knowledge and insights we need to improve our practice and come ever closer to the goal of universal student success. As with many simple ideas, the ramifications can be huge. The greatest virtue of action research is its potential for radically transforming the conditions of work for the classroom teacher, specifically those conditions that when left unaddressed will frustrate and burn out our best and brightest.

In settings where the norms and practices that are supportive of action research have been institutionalized, teachers are achieving success, as demonstrated by continuous improved performance by students and a reduction in the achievement gap (Little, 1982; Rosenholtz, 1985). Better yet, in these settings, teachers are finding their work more satisfying, more energizing, and less guilt producing.

In the chapters that follow, we will explore numerous strategies used by teachers to accomplish the four stages of the action research process. You will encounter concrete examples of how teachers have worked through each of the stages and explore strategies with step-by-step instructions and sample materials that you can use as is or adapt for use with your own action research. As we work our way through the process, we will continue to return to the working conditions issues (complexity, time, and support) and explore ways that the habits of action research could help you manage them.

■ KEY TERMS AND CONCEPTS

Action Research

At the start of this chapter, we offered a definition of action research that indicated that it is an investigation conducted *by the person or the people empowered to take action concerning their own actions, for the purpose of improving their future actions.* It would be helpful to expand on this so that we can clearly distinguish *action* research from other forms of scientific or educational research. The best way to decide if an inquiry qualifies as action research is to ask three questions about the proposed study. If the answer to all three is "yes," then the inquiry justifiably fits under an action research umbrella. If the answer to any of the questions is "no," then while it might be an area worth investigating, action research isn't the appropriate approach. These are the questions:

1. Is the Focus on Your Professional Action?

If you are studying your own work, then the answer to this question is clearly "yes." In addition, if you are studying something that you are considering making part of your work in the future, then the answer can also be "yes." According to Kemmis and McTaggart (1988), there are three types of action that can legitimately serve as foci for action research:

Research of action (past action): In this case, the action being studied has been completed (e.g., an evaluation study).

Research in action (present action): In this case, the action is underway (e.g., a monitoring study).

Research for action (future action): In this case, the action will occur in the near future (e.g., evaluating materials for adoption).

2. Are You Empowered to Adjust Future Action Based on the Results?

This question pertains to your sphere of influence. Most teachers are free to adjust their instructional strategies as they deem appropriate. Therefore, considering an investigation into a new approach for instruction justifies a "yes" to this question. This is because the teacher-researchers are free to change their teaching based on the data they gather. Likewise, members of a school improvement team are often empowered to make changes for their entire school and therefore could answer this question with a "yes" for a study that was examining a schoolwide issue. If circumstances prevent you from being able to make changes, regardless of what the data reveal, you will have to answer "no" to this question.

3. Is Improvement Possible?

Although we all know that research for its own sake is a worthy pursuit, the only justification for practicing educators to invest valuable time in research is if the inquiry holds promise for helping them be more successful with their teaching. If you hold serious doubts that performance can in fact improve in a particular area, then you would be wise not to embark on action research concerning it.

To recap, an investigation qualifies as action research if it pertains to one's professional action, focuses on an aspect of one's work where one has a significant degree of control, and where (with enough information) improvement can be expected to occur.

The Four Stages

As you pursue the action research process through its four sequential stages, you will find that each stage is designed to help you answer a key question.

Stage 1: Clarifying Vision and Targets

Key question: What do I want to accomplish?

In Stage 1, action researchers clearly enunciate their goals, clarify each of the subskills or attributes that contribute to success for each goal, and specify detailed criteria that can be used with validity and reliability to document improvement. Ways to accomplish the tasks of Stage 1 and answer its question are examined in Chapters 2 and 3.

Stage 2: Articulating Theory

Key question: What do I believe is the approach with the greatest potential for achieving my goal(s)?

In this stage, action researchers articulate a detailed rationale for proceeding in a particular fashion. Earlier we talked about the many factors that need to be considered when making a lesson-planning decision. When there is no proven best way to accomplish a goal, professionals will often pursue alternative approaches that they deem theoretically sound. It is in Stage 2 that action researchers engage in a deliberate planning process that involves examining and incorporating all of the dynamic relationships between the relevant factors or variables that might influence success in realizing the vision or targets identified in Stage 1. We work through the processes for articulating your own theory of action and answering Stage 2's key question in Chapters 4 and 5.

Stage 3: Implementing Action and Collecting Data

Key question: What data will I need to collect to understand the efficacy and workings of my theory of action?

This is the portion of the action research process that takes place during actual teaching, our professional action. It is here that we carry through on our theory of action while systematically compiling information (data) to help us understand what is going on, both above and below the surface. This is where we determine what is being accomplished and the relationship between the actions being taken and the results being obtained. Work on Stage 3 begins in Chapter 6, where you learn how to generate a set of research questions to guide your study. Then in Chapter 7, you learn how to develop a viable data-collection plan aimed at producing valid and reliable answers for those research questions.

Stage 4: Reflecting on the Data and Planning Informed Action

Key question: Based on this data, how should I adjust my future actions (teaching)?

Stage 4 is where we complete the first lap around the action research cycle. It is here that action researchers return and revisit their visions or targets (Stage 1) as well as their previous thinking on the best way to realize that vision (Stage 2). Then based on data regarding the impact of their actions (Stage 3) and an analysis of those data, action researchers produce a revised theory of action, which then forms the basis for future action. Figure 1.1 illustrates the cyclical nature of the work accomplished through the four stages.

The Two Categories of Action Research

Action research, like most types of inquiry, is generally undertaken for one of two purposes:

- To determine what is currently occurring
- To test a hypothesis (theory)

When researchers seek to understand what is occurring, they are engaging in what is called *descriptive research.* When the research is primarily concerned with testing a hypothesis, the inquiry is called *quasi-experimental research.* (The qualifier "quasi" is used here because in the social sciences, it is both ethically and practically impossible to implement a classic experimental design, since that would require a control group. Research that seeks to test a hypothesis without a control group is classified as quasi-experimental. This problem will be discussed in greater length in Chapter 7.)

Figure 1.1   Action Research Cycle

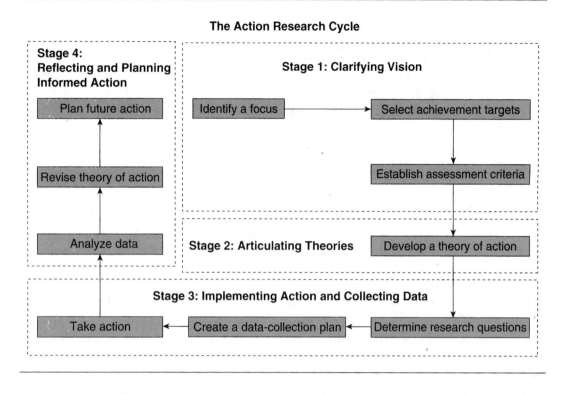

Quasi-Experimental Research

As teachers, we are frequently involved in quasi-experimental research, although most of us haven't been in the habit of documenting our studies. Every day, teachers make use of the best approaches they know. Yet it is a very rare day when all the students in a class accomplish everything they possibly could. More often than not, when we reflect on why a student or group of students hasn't succeeded, it triggers some creative thinking. We find ourselves asking, "What if . . . ?" When we are pondering the what-ifs, we are considering ideas or hypotheses that we might investigate. If we decide to attempt something new, we are saying that we believe this approach is likely to produce superior outcomes than the ones we had obtained before. When you decide to focus on the use of a new or modified idea, your research becomes a quasi-experimental study of the adequacy of that idea, or what is called in this text, your *theory of action.* Because of the dynamic and ever-changing nature of teaching, it shouldn't be surprising that this is the most common form of action research.

Descriptive Research

There are many times when we find ourselves concerned about something occurring in our classrooms, with our kids, or in our schools. We know that we want to do something about the problem, but we don't feel we currently understand the issue in the context of our school or classroom well enough to design an effective strategy for improvement. When this occurs, our ultimate goal is no different than that of educators who have decided to conduct quasi-experimental research. All desire to learn what we need to know to improve performance; it is only the focus that is different. While the lens of the quasi-experimental researchers is trained on the efficacy of a particular innovation (their theory of action) and its impact, the lens of the descriptive researchers is on the system or approach that is currently in place (the *operative* theory of action) and trying to understand its workings. Whatever the focus of your study, be it your theory or the operative theory, at Stage 4, all action researchers end up doing the same thing: producing a plan for future action based on data regarding what occurred in the past. Figure 1.2 contrasts these two types of research across the four stages of the action research process.

It is worth noting that these two categories of research (quasi-experimental and descriptive) are not mutually exclusive. Sometimes they even occur simultaneously. In Chapters 7 and 8 we will explore an example of action research being conducted by a hypothetical fifth-grade teacher, Ms. Pioneer. She is implementing a theory of her own design. Her theory of action involves making use of cooperative learning and multimedia technology in her teaching of social studies content. The major thrust of her study is quasi-experimental, as she wants to understand if and how her theory of action is succeeding in furthering her goals. But at the same time, she will be conducting a study within a study. This is because she has a particular student in class, Joann Heathrow, who is a real handful. Joann hasn't experienced much success in Ms. Pioneer's class, nor has she been successful in any other teacher's classroom. Ms. Pioneer would like to see Joann doing better but has been unable to develop confidence that any specific strategy will help this ADHD child succeed with her curriculum. She is interested in examining Joann's experience in her class (a descriptive action research study), not primarily to understand her program but to better understand how the instructional environment and Joann interact with each other. Ms. Pioneer's hope is that after gathering more data on Joann's experience, she will be better able to develop a theory of action for helping Joann achieve success within the classroom.

It should be noted that *descriptive* and *quasi-experimental* are not simply synonyms for *qualitative* and *quantitative* research. While qualitative research methods are used to paint a robust picture of a phenomenon, they are also frequently used by action researchers conducting quasi-experimental studies. For example, in trying to determine the impact of a new innovative reading program (a quasi-experimental study), I might use qualitative data drawn from student reading journals and observational notes. Likewise, a team conducting a descriptive study aimed at understanding the climate at their school might use a survey where students and teachers rate attributes of the school on a 10-point scale (a qualitative method). Most action research studies end up making use of both qualitative and quantitative data-collection methods.

■ UNIVERSAL STUDENT SUCCESS

As mentioned earlier, most teachers approach their work with very high expectations. Ultimately, our goal is to have all students doing their very best work and becoming as skillful as possible. This is not unlike physicians approaching their work with the goal of curing *every* condition and helping *every* patient live a long and vigorous life.

Realistically, we know that this can't and won't happen all at once, if ever. Rome wasn't built in a day, and all human illness will not be eradicated in one fell swoop. Likewise, figuring out how to assist all learners to realize their potential will take time. But as inquiring professionals, we want to be continuously advancing our

Figure 1.2 Comparison of Four-Stage Action Research Process Between Quasi-Experimental and Descriptive Research

Stage	Quasi-Experimental Research	Descriptive Research
1: Clarifying vision and targets	The researchers draw clear and robust pictures of the desired outcomes. They attempt to visualize and imagine success in as much detail as possible.	Same as quasi-experimental
	The researchers identify the subcomponents of their vision. For each critical component, they decide on criteria to assess changes occurring with that component.	
2: Articulating theory	The researchers consider their own experience as well as the experience of others attempting to realize the vision and its components.	The researchers consider their own experience as well as the experience of others attempting to realize the vision and its components.
	Based on this examination, the researchers develop a new theory of action that involves a modification of past practice and holds promise for improving performance.	After reflecting on personal experience and the experience of others, the researchers conclude that more information (on what is occurring and how things are working) would be helpful.
	The new theory of action becomes the focus of study.	The researchers clarify the operative theory of action (what is now being done), which becomes the focus of their study.
3: Implementation, collecting data	The researchers examine the new theory of action and determine a set of questions that they need or want to have answered.	The researchers examine the operative theory of action, looking for aspects of the theory (i.e., strategies, materials, outcomes, etc.) whose effects need to be better understood.
	The researchers develop a viable plan for collecting the necessary data.	The researchers develop a viable plan for collecting the data needed to illuminate the implementation of the operative theory.
	The researchers implement the new theory of action and collect the data as outlined in their plan.	The researchers collect the data as indicated in their plan.
4: Reflecting on data, planning informed action	The researchers compile and summarize the data collected in Step 3 and generate a list of findings.	Same as quasi-experimental
	Using these findings, the researchers summarize any insights gained regarding the realization of the vision.	
	The researchers develop a revised theory of action incorporating new and relevant insights.	
	The researchers make plans to implement the revised theory of action.	

wisdom on what it will take to realize universal success. In the next chapter, we begin working on Stage 1, where you are asked to take stock of your vision for student success. To do this, you articulate a vision of truly outstanding performance so that you will be able to incrementally measure your success as you move ever closer to assisting every student accomplish all that he or she can. When we use the term *universal student success,* that is precisely what we mean. It is that Promised Land that we are always reaching for, that wondrous time and place where all of us educators are in possession of all that needs to be known to maximize the learning for all of our students.

With this as our goal, it is likely that this collective search for answers to the perplexing problems of teaching and learning will keep us occupied for the rest of our careers. However, as long as we are purposefully engaged in the action research process and see evidence that we are continuing to learn our way forward along the road to universal student success, we can anticipate a career of celebrations, when we can stop and collectively acknowledge each breakthrough being made along the way.

2

Finding a Focus

Every educator and any parent with his or her eyes open can see how demanding teaching has become. There simply aren't enough hours in the day for teachers to accomplish all the things on their plates, much less attend to their families, their mental health, and the everyday chores of modern life. But even with all that is required of them, teachers regularly volunteer to abuse themselves and put in countless hours and burn an infinite number of calories trying to generate improved performance in areas that are a personal priority. Consider, for example, the time spent by English teachers responding individually to student work or the time coaches spend analyzing game film in preparation for the next contest. When educators have reason to believe that their efforts will produce a payoff in student performance, they willingly and excitedly invest whatever it takes to make success a reality.

Action research has been proven to be a productive strategy for improving teaching and learning (Hord, 1997; Joyce & Calhoun, 1996). Furthermore, educators have found conducting action research to be both enjoyable and rewarding (Caro-Bruce & Zeichner, 1998). While this is most often the case, these positive outcomes aren't guaranteed.

ZEROING IN ON YOUR PRIORITIES ■

Research has demonstrated clearly that the intellectual and affective benefits of action research correspond directly to the focus of the research (Sagor & Curley, 1991). If a teacher's action research addresses an issue that is of significant personal or professional importance, then invariably, the time spent conducting the research is considered well spent. However, if the issue under investigation turns out to be peripheral to the central concerns of the researcher, then even the smallest investment of energy is resented. This is completely logical. With time in short supply, any time spent on one endeavor is time that is not available for other things. Inviting teachers to pursue anything they lack passion for is encouraging them to invest in frustration and guilt.

For this reason, the selection of a focus for one's action research is a step that mustn't be taken lightly. Prematurely rushing to a research focus may be the single worst thing a prospective action researcher can do. While there is no best way to choose a focus for inquiry, there are a number of strategies that have proven helpful. We explore a few of these approaches as we get started on *Stage 1: Clarifying the Vision and Targets* of the action research process.

The remainder of this chapter will be devoted to five specific strategies that have assisted educational action researchers in identifying high-priority, meaningful topics for study. These are *reflective writing, journaling, reflective interviewing, analytic discourse,* and *team reflection.* I suggest that you read through the entire chapter and then decide which of these approaches would work best for you; then use it (or them) to narrow your focus before going on to Chapter 3.

■ USING REFLECTIVE WRITING TO FIND A FOCUS

The daily to-do list for most teachers is huge. The have-to's are so numerous that oftentimes they crowd out the want-to's. Worse, the absence of time for meaningful reflection often results in busy educators losing touch with their own priority want-to's. Occasionally, it has been such a long time since teachers have had the luxury of reflecting on what really matters to them that personal priorities no longer even show up on their to-do lists.

As an action researcher, you will be well served to call a time-out at this point so that you can reconnect with your own priorities. While most everyone agrees with the need for and value of reflection, the pace of school life leaves little opportunity to engage in acts of purposeful reflection. It is often necessary to shut out all other distractions so that there is time and space for the quality reflection necessary for zeroing in on a meaningful topic for action research.

This is the primary virtue of the *reflective writing* process. Composing our thoughts and generating a narrative necessarily consumes all of a person's available intellectual energy and consequently provides the concentration needed for reflecting on a potential action research focus.

While no one questions that writing is a marvelous way to become focused, it is frequently difficult to get started. Many teachers who have used the writing process with their students have found that an effective way of helping someone get over writer's block is through the use of prewriting exercises. It is not uncommon for teachers to invest several class periods just helping their students get ready to write. This isn't just a need of novice writers. Many professional authors spend days, weeks, or even months reflecting and mentally working over an issue before they first approach the keyboard.

Since it can be difficult to get started with reflective writing and since time is usually in short supply, it is a good idea to create boundaries prior to starting. Boundaries help with concentration and jumpstart the process. An effective way to create boundaries for reflective writing is through the use of a prompt. Any prompt that helps you focus on your professional priorities will work.

The prompts that I've found most helpful are ones that ask me to engage in an imaginary conversation with a significant other. I suspect there are several reasons why imagination and fantasy are so helpful in stimulating my reflections. The most important is that sometimes, especially when I am feeling depressed or worn down, I start losing confidence. But as long as I'm breathing, I will likely never lose my innate human capacity to dream. There is, however, another more important reason why the use of imagination and fantasy is productive for an action researcher. When I'm dreaming, I am no longer limited by the constraints of what is realistic; instead, I get a chance to dwell on the fantastic.

One writing prompt that I have found particularly helpful is the following:

Imagine it is the close of this school year. The year that just ended has been, without a doubt, the most satisfying of your entire career. It has been so good that you are actually feeling depressed that you won't get a chance to teach your kids for nearly 3 months! You leave school on that last day positively glowing. You are practically walking 2 feet off the ground, feeling terrific about your work, about the profession you are a part of, and about the impact your work is having on your students.

Returning home, you find yourself talking on the phone with an old friend. Your friend asks how the year went. You reply that it was unequivocally the best school year ever, exceeding even your wildest expectations! Your friend then asks, what specifically did you and your students do and what was accomplished that made it such a wonderful year?

What do you hear yourself saying in return?

Write your answer in as much detail as possible. Write in the conversational voice you would likely use with a friend (when professional language and jargon are avoided, most of us tend to become more creative and our ideas flow more easily).

Let's now imagine that I am a middle school social studies teacher who has just written in response to that prompt. I could well have written something like this:

Teaching social studies to eighth graders had become such a battle for me. Over the years, I became used to seeing the same pattern: My students came to class on Day 1 expecting to hate it. They saw no purpose in studying government and were sure that this was going to be the most boring material they would ever have to endure. Truthfully, I was starting to dread the start of each new class. I once read where at the beginning of each term, the students and the teacher negotiate a treaty. In essence, the kids offer to trade their cooperation and positive behavior in exchange for lower expectations from the teacher. Each year I was seeing myself giving away more and more in these exchanges. It had actually gotten to the point that sometimes I wasn't quite sure why I was teaching this stuff at all, as it seemed the less I covered, the happier it made the kids.

What was even worse was dealing with their cynicism. Heck, the reason I majored in political science and decided to teach social studies was because I love our political system and believe deeply in the democratic process. For the past few years, the message I've been receiving from my students was that I was

---

(Continued)

(Continued)

just another adult, "preaching this nonsense"! In every way possible, from their behavior to the things they said in class and wrote in their papers, they consistently told me that they believed you couldn't fight city hall. In their minds, those in power, be it their parents, the school administration, or the holders of political offices, would continue to do just as they pleased. The only choice they felt they had now or, for that matter, would have in the future was to avoid making waves or to get their needs met by cheating or conniving. I'm telling you, it was getting so depressing to hear such fatalism from the lips of 13-year-olds that I was seriously thinking of giving up teaching.

Well, last summer, not knowing what else to do, I decided to try something radical. It seemed that every book I'd read said that middle school students thrive when doing hands-on activities. All the consultants say that kids learn best and enjoy it most when they are actively involved. It all sounded good, but it seemed irrelevant to my subject. According to the state regulations, my kids had to learn about the United States Constitution, the separation of powers, and the three levels of government. What was I going to do, put them in a time capsule and ship them back to 1776?

As nothing else was working, I decided to throw caution to the wind and do just that. . . . Well, almost. Since we couldn't do time travel, I did the next best thing. I told them that if they felt oppressed by the current system, they were in the same boat as the colonists. Once they secured their independence from the British Crown, the colonists faced another problem: figuring out an effective way to govern themselves. At that point, the ball was in the colonists' court. Could the founders actually create something superior to the one they so detested? This was when I took my big-time risk. I granted them their independence.

I told them, "I surrender. Your revolution has succeeded; you are now free from my expectations, my curriculum, and my system! It's now up to you to decide how to take care of the business of eighth-grade government!" Of course, I also reminded them that if they didn't pass the district social studies level test, they would have to deal with the consequences. But I told them, as free citizens, this was now their responsibility.

Well, after a few awkward days, all five of my eighth-grade civics classes asked me if I had any advice to give. Breathing a sigh of relief, I told them what the representatives of the 13 original states had decided at this point: They committed themselves to the work of designing a constitution which laid out what they wanted to accomplish and the processes they would use to get things done.

To make a long story short, the kids took the bait. They asked me what a constitution was, how it worked, and how one could be created. The next thing I knew, they were developing a parallel constitution for the eighth-grade civics classes. Each of my five classes became an independent state, and together they designed a constitution that governed "our" republic as well as preserved "states' rights" for each of the independent classes. Later, each class designed its own "state" constitution. Before I knew it, the kids had designed a system remarkably similar to the three-tiered U.S. system of government. We had three levels: Inside each class, cooperative learning teams worked like local governments, each class behaved like a state, and the United Classes of East-Side Middle School performed just like a federal government.

> Well, the year seemed to fly by. The kids had a ball and worked harder than any group of kids I had ever had before. I stopped assigning readings from the textbook, although many times I noticed kids looking stuff up when they needed it to solve an emerging problem. Two weeks before the district exam, I provided a copy of the same study guide I had used in past years and left them on their own to prepare. I was amazed!! They did better than any group of students I'd had before. If you can believe it, my kids tied for the highest scores in the district.
>
> Not only did they learn the material, but also they loved the class. The best part was that on my end-of-year questionnaire, 90% of my students said that social studies was their favorite subject.
>
> I'm jazzed. This experience has given me a whole new lease on my teaching life. . . . I think I'll stick with it!!

Notice that I truly let my imagination flow. I didn't get bogged down in educational lingo or shorthand; I simply fantasized what heaven would look and feel like for me. Later you may want to try your hand with this same prompt. The Reflective Writing Worksheet (Figure 2.1) has been provided for your use when drafting your vision of the Promised Land.

Most state laws or district evaluation policies require teachers to set goals at the start of each school year. While on the surface these policies appear rational, rarely do they result in the development of meaningful goals that hold emotional significance for the authors. This happens largely because the drafting of these goals occurs devoid of meaningful reflection. In all likelihood, the narrative you wrote (or will write) on Figure 2.1 will bring to the surface goals that matter more to you personally and professionally than the often perfunctory goals that you are required to generate as part of the evaluation process. Hopefully, your narrative brought to life things that *you* would really love to see accomplished. My narrative certainly did. It contained a vision that, if it were realized, would have made me a very happy and fulfilled educator.

While written narratives are helpful in illuminating an overall focus, they are often too general. One way to sharpen your focus and to gain the precision that will be needed for research is to systematically dissect the narrative you wrote. This is done by looking at the big picture contained in the reflective writing and then identifying the specific outcomes that contributed to the realization of the overall vision. From this point on, we will refer to these specific outcomes as the action researcher's *priority achievement targets.* The range of categories and nature of achievement targets is broad. The three categories of foci that I find emerge most frequently for teacher-researchers are the following:

- Performance targets
- Process targets
- Program targets

Performance targets relate to what students are expected to gain from our actions. There are many synonyms for *performance targets:* Some states call them content standards, essential learnings, curriculum goals, and so on. A well-stated performance target can help us focus on what students should know, should be able to do and/or choose to do, and may even cause us to look for changes in how

Figure 2.1   Reflective Writing Worksheet

Imagine it is the end of the next school year. The past year has been, without a doubt, the most satisfying of your entire career. You left school glowing with good feelings about your work, your profession, and about the impact your work is having on students.

A close friend has just asked you how your year went, and you reply that it was the best ever. When your friend asks you to share what specifically occurred that made you feel this way, what do you reply?

_____

_____

_____

_____

_____

_____

_____

_____

_____

_____

_____

_____

_____

_____

_____

_____

_____

_____

_____

_____

Copyright © 2005 Corwin Press. All rights reserved. Reprinted from *The Action Research Handbook: A Four-Step Process for Educators and School Teams,* by Richard Sagor. Thousand Oaks, CA: Corwin Press, www .corwinpress.com. Reproduction authorized only for the local school site that has purchased this book.

students should feel if the instruction was successful. There are four major categories of performance targets:

- Cognitive: What students know
- Demonstrative: What students can do
- Behavioral: What they choose to do
- Affective: How they feel about themselves and the situation they are part of

Process targets relate to techniques or strategies that we want to be part of our teaching repertoire. While performance targets refer to what students can do (or will be able to do better), process targets focus on specific improvements that we would like to see in ourselves (i.e., our teaching skills). For example, I might want to improve my ability to conduct classroom discussions or become better at modeling problem-solving strategies.

Program targets focus on outcomes for an entire classroom or school as an organization. In many ways, program targets are similar to performance targets, but with program targets, we are primarily concerned with the impact on the group or the organization as opposed to the impact on any one individual participant. For example, a program target might refer to the impact a program will have on school climate, faculty morale, or parental involvement.

The Target Identification Form (Figure 2.2) is designed to help you identify your priority achievement targets through a review of your reflective narrative. Use this form to locate and synthesize the specific targets (components or outcomes) that, when taken together, contributed to your imaginary most satisfying year. For example, the priority achievement targets that contributed to my great year are shown in Figure 2.3.

Once you have identified your priority achievement targets, you are getting closer to finding a focus for action research. All you need to do is preface each of your bulleted targets with the phrase, "Investigating how to produce . . . ," and you will have a list of potentially meaningful foci for action research. What makes these good topics for action research is that they focus on the three essentials:

a. Your actions

b. Improved performance

c. An issue that matters to *you*

USING A JOURNAL TO IDENTIFY ACTION RESEARCH FOCI

Using a journal to find an action research focus has many of the same virtues as reflective writing. The major difference is that journaling spreads reflections over a period of time. What is so good about extending the time frame for reflection is that it allows us to observe patterns and trends in our priority concerns and passions.

Some teachers are already in the journaling habit. However, for many, keeping a journal is not part of a daily routine and probably isn't very likely to become so in the future. This is another instance when establishing boundaries is helpful for structuring work. If the discipline of journal writing isn't part of your nature, this is another occasion when boundary setting can limit the time needed for this exercise while not reducing its value.

Figure 2.2 Target Identification Form

Reread your report of your marvelous year, asking the following questions (write your responses under each one):

What specific accomplishments did you observe students making (e.g., greater responsibility, more precision in their writing, improved thinking skills)? These are *performance targets*.

_____

_____

_____

_____

_____

What specific changes did you observe in your teaching behavior (e.g., more use of project-based learning, improved questioning skills, more personalized instruction)? These are *process targets*.

_____

_____

_____

_____

_____

What specific changes did you observe in your classroom (e.g., greater sense of community, higher levels of on-task behavior, less misbehavior)? These are *program targets*.

_____

_____

_____

_____

_____

Copyright © 2005 Corwin Press. All rights reserved. Reprinted from *The Action Research Handbook: A Four-Step Process for Educators and School Teams,* by Richard Sagor. Thousand Oaks, CA: Corwin Press, www.corwinpress.com. Reproduction authorized only for the local school site that has purchased this book.

Figure 2.3 My Great Year: Priority Achievement Targets

- High scores on district social studies exam (achievement target)
- Conceptual understanding of separation of powers (achievement target)
- Conceptual understanding of levels of government (achievement target)
- Enjoyment of social studies (achievement target)
- Positive classroom behavior (achievement target)
- Increased skills in managing hands-on learning (process target)
- Increased skills in facilitating rather than directing learning (process target)
- Improved classroom climate (program target)
- Increased students' liking of social studies (program target)

Boundaries or guidelines that I have found useful when using a journal to pinpoint action research foci include the following:

- Two weeks (maximum) of daily journal entries
- Approximately 10 minutes of writing per day (15-minute maximum)
- Responding to the same prompt each day

When using journal writing to find a research focus, it is wise to make use of a consistent prompt. Writing to the same topic each day creates boundaries and make it much easier to analyze your reflections once you are finished. One versatile and productive prompt I have found follows.

What occurred in class today that was significant for me?
By *significant*, I mean what *went well*, what *went poorly*, what *surprised* me, and *what questions* did I end the day with?

A hypothetical journal entry from a fifth-grade teacher follows, written during the first 2 weeks of school.

I felt a little guilty about today's science lesson. It being only the second week of school, I thought I should be presenting this material myself. Having the students learn the material through the jigsaw activity felt like I was cheating, taking the easy way out. But by not having the responsibility of directly teaching the material, I think I was more relaxed than I usually am when I have to teach science. And the fact that I wasn't stressed was a real plus. I moved around the room and interacted with a number of kids I hadn't spoken with much up until now. Maybe I'm trying to convince myself of something, but I think *my* being relaxed was contagious. It seemed to lighten the mood for everyone. I'll be curious to see if this same thing happens next time I have them doing group work.

Journaling is an especially good way to find a topic for a collaborative or team action research project. When using this process for this purpose, every member of the team writes to the same prompt over the same time period. Later, the team looks for patterns in the issues and concerns that came to light across the team members.

What I like most about the journal process is how much material is produced in so little time. After a mere 2 weeks, you will have produced 10 separate journal entries. Now consider this: If you were planning on doing action research collaboratively (for example, with 10 other teachers from your department), 2 weeks of journaling would have yielded 100 real-time teacher reflections.

In Chapter 7, journaling is revisited as a data-collection strategy. Perhaps you can already see what a powerful data-gathering tool journal writing can be. One hundred individual journal entries generated by people working on a regular basis with the students attending a single school, each one focused on classroom issues that are significant to them, would constitute a goldmine of data. And collecting all that treasure would take just 10 minutes per day.

Returning to our original purpose, which was using journals to identify a focus for research, your 10 entries may appear to be creating too much material. However, once you spend a little bit of time analyzing the entries, you will easily be able to spot an issue or issues with personal meaning that should be well worth spending your time researching.

If you choose to use the journaling strategy, you will likely want to create forms like the Action Research Journal pages shown in Figure 2.4, to collect the journal entries that you and any other members of your action research team generate.

Once you have collected all of your journal entries, it is time to look for patterns. The questions found on the Journal Analysis Form (Figure 2.5) will help you identify recurrent themes that surfaced during the 2-week writing period. Now, use the same process that was used with the narrative visions: Preface each of your items with the phrase, "Investigating how to produce. . . ." You now have a list of personally meaningful foci for action research.

■ REFLECTIVE INTERVIEWS

Another approach for identifying a meaningful focus is the reflective interview, a process where we make use of the ear of a colleague as we verbally articulate our thinking on an issue or concern. Most often, the reflective interview is carried out in pairs. Participants take turns discussing a matter of personal concern regarding their work. Each person has a predetermined amount of time to talk about his or her issue. I like to allocate 15 minutes per participant. This way, in a scheduled 45-minute meeting, each person can have a full 15 minutes for his or her issue, with another 15 minutes available for clarification and summarizing.

Reflective interviews give the action researchers a chance to hear their own ideas as they are spoken and as they are heard through the schooled ear of a colleague. It is important to understand that the reflective interview *is not a discussion.* If someone were to track the talking with a stopwatch during a reflective interview, the interviewee would be seen using at least 90% of the allocated airtime. The only occasion when an interviewer should be talking is when he or she is confused and needs clarification or if the interviewee seems to have run out of things to say. In such a case,

Figure 2.4   Action Research Journal

Date: _____

Make 10 copies of this sheet for your daily journal entries. Beginning on the agreed-on start date, _____, keep a journal for 10 consecutive days. Do your writing after the school day has ended and when you have 15 minutes of uninterrupted quiet time.

Be sure and place the date on the top of the page, and write in response to the prompt decided on (for instance, *What went well, what went poorly, what surprised me, and what questions did I end today with?*).

Copyright © 2005 Corwin Press. All rights reserved. Reprinted from *The Action Research Handbook: A Four-Step Process for Educators and School Teams,* by Richard Sagor. Thousand Oaks, CA: Corwin Press, www .corwinpress.com. Reproduction authorized only for the local school site that has purchased this book.

Figure 2.5   Journal Analysis Form

Read through your 10 journal entries in chronological order, with a pad of paper by your side. Whenever you come upon something that concerned you, pleased you, surprised you, or raised a question for you, write it down. If you see a reference to the same concern, satisfying experience, surprise, or question on another day, put a check mark by that item on your list.

   Now prioritize the items on your list in descending order of how many times each showed up during your 2 weeks of journaling.

_____

_____

_____

_____

_____

For each item, ask the following questions:

1. Does this item have an impact on a student outcome that matters to me (keep in mind an outcome can be academic, behavioral, or affective)? List the items that you responded to with a *yes*:

_____

_____

_____

_____

_____

2. Do I understand this issue or phenomenon as well as I'd like to? List the items that you responded to with a *no*:

_____

_____

_____

_____

_____

_____

The items listed may be good candidates for action research foci.

Copyright © 2005 Corwin Press. All rights reserved. Reprinted from *The Action Research Handbook: A Four-Step Process for Educators and School Teams,* by Richard Sagor. Thousand Oaks, CA: Corwin Press, www.corwinpress.com. Reproduction authorized only for the local school site that has purchased this book.

Figure 2.6   Reflective Interview Meeting Agenda

0:00–0:15

Interview 1

The first person takes 15 minutes to talk about a work issue. The issue discussed must meet the following criteria:

- It is matter of significant interest (something one is excited or concerned about).
- Performance in this area can be influenced by the work of the interviewee.
- Improvement in this area could potentially be made.

0:15–0:17

The interviewer takes 2 minutes to summarize what was heard. The interviewer prefaces the comments with, "I understood you to say . . ."

0:17–0:22

The interviewee and interviewer clarify their understanding of the interviewee's issue.

0:23–0:38

Interview 2

The second person takes 15 minutes to talk about a work issue. The issue discussed must meet the following criteria:

- It is matter of significant interest (something one is excited or concerned about).
- Performance in this area can be influenced by the work of the interviewee.
- Improvement in this area could potentially be made.

0:38–0:40

The interviewer takes 2 minutes to summarize what was heard. The interviewer prefaces the comments with, "I understood you to say . . ."

0:40–0:45

The interviewee and interviewer clarify their understanding of the interviewee's issue.

---

the job of the interviewer is to say something to get the interviewee started again, for example by asking,

- Has this concerned you for a long time?
- What things have you tried?
- What would you like to do about this?

Figure 2.6 shows an example of a meeting agenda designed for paired reflective interviewing.

To recap, the purpose of the reflective interview is the same as for reflective writing and journaling: to clarify a focus for research that is

1. Of significant personal professional concern

2. Within the researcher's personal sphere of influence

3. An area where improvement is possible

Frequently, the simple act of conducting the reflective interview followed by filling in the target form (Figure 2.2) is all that is required to identify a focus for research. Other times, it is helpful to follow the reflective interview with a few minutes of reflective writing using a prompt like the one in Figure 2.1, and then proceeding to fill out the target form.

■ ANALYTIC DISCOURSE

The analytic discourse is a close cousin of the reflective interview. However, in this case, a panel of three to six colleagues conducts the interview, all of whom share an interest in or concern about the same general topic.

An analytic discourse generally follows this format:

1. *Presentation of issue.* The action researcher takes 5 minutes to outline an area of interest.

2. *Clarifying questions.* Each panel member gets to ask for clarification of anything that is not clear.

3. *Probing Questions.* Panel members ask questions designed to push the researcher to explore and enunciate a deeper understanding of the area of concern. The types of questions asked can include things such as, *What do you think explains this? What things have been tried to address this in the past, here or elsewhere? What would you like to see happen?*

When conducting an analytic discourse, three ground rules must be followed by the interview panel. These rules are designed to ensure that the researcher-interviewee arrives at a deeper personal understanding of the issue. The ground rules are

1. *Questions only; no comments* (the goal is clarifying the researcher-interviewee's understanding of the issue)

2. *No critical comments* (the purpose is not to debate but to enhance understanding)

3. *No suggestions* (it is the job of the researcher-interviewee to make proposals)

At the conclusion of an analytic discourse, use the achievement target worksheet (Figure 2.2) to fine-tune a potential focus or foci for action research.

■ TEAM REFLECTION

Many times, a work group (a grade-level team, a department, or a cross-district group) will want to work together on a collaborative action research project. One good strategy for finding a meaningful group topic combines the attributes of the reflective writing process and the reflective interview. The focus form (Figure 2.7) is a worksheet that has been used by grade-level and departmental teams for selecting a collaborative action research focus.

Each person spends 15 minutes personally answering the four questions on the focus form. After everyone has had a chance to do their reflective writing, a 1-hour team meeting is called. The first half of the meeting is spent with random pairs conducting reflective interviews. Once every person has had a chance to verbally

Figure 2.7   Collaborative Action Research Group Focus Worksheet

Group: _____

Purpose: Conducting action research collaboratively has proven to be both rewarding and productive for teachers, *if* the focus for the research meets four conditions: it is sharply focused, pertains to the realization of a shared vision, focuses on an area where improvement could and should be made, and makes change within the group's sphere of influence. Using this form will help your group find a meaningful focus for group work.

Instructions: Find a time and place where you can allocate 15 uninterrupted minutes for writing and thinking about the work your group will be engaging in next year.

Check the time and begin responding to the four questions on these sheets. Stick with the task until the 15 minutes are up. If your thinking stalls, continue to reflect on the issues, as new thoughts and ideas will likely emerge if you give it time. If you need more space, write on the back of these sheets or add paper as necessary—the more elaboration the better!

   After 15 minutes of reflection and writing, your work is done. Please return the completed form to your group leader.

Here are the questions:

1. What are the priority issues, projects, and programs that we should be working on collaboratively next year?

   _____

   _____

   _____

   _____

2. Which of the listed issues, projects, or programs is the highest priority to you? Why? (Please expand your answer as much as possible.)

   _____

   _____

   _____

   _____

3. If the group succeeded with this endeavor beyond your wildest expectations, what would the results look like? (Please be as specific as possible.)

   _____

   _____

   _____

   _____

4. What factors, issues, or obstacles have gotten in the way of achieving this extraordinary level of success (#3, above) in the past?

   _____

   _____

   _____

   _____

Copyright © 2005 Corwin Press. All rights reserved. Reprinted from *The Action Research Handbook: A Four-Step Process for Educators and School Teams,* by Richard Sagor. Thousand Oaks, CA: Corwin Press, www.corwinpress.com. Reproduction authorized only for the local school site that has purchased this book.

share his or her ideas, the entire group convenes and collects the common issues, ideas, and targets that were identified in the reflective interviews. Achievement targets that surfaced in multiple interviews become possible foci for a group action research project.

There is no one technique to choose a focus for action research. Any one of the strategies discussed in this chapter or a combination of them should help an educator select a direction for research that is worth his or her time. Whatever approach you decide to use, it is imperative to *stop before proceeding any farther* to ask yourself or your team, "Is this topic really worth an investment of my or our precious time and energy?" Put another way, you might want to ask,

> If time is spent pursuing improved action in the pursuit of this target or these targets, and consequently, if insights are gained that enable more success, will this time have been well spent?

If you can answer that question with an emphatic "yes," you are ready to proceed.

3

Refining the Focus

Recreational travel to exotic and rarely visited destinations can be exhilarating. The anticipation that builds for months before your departure can be nearly as much fun as the trip itself. While there is no question that planning a trip takes significant time, it is frequently the single most important thing that you can do to guarantee that the trip will end up a success.

One of the aspects of pretravel planning that makes it so much fun is that there are few, if any, constraints on our imaginations. As we envision what it will be like to go where we have never gone before, we are free to fantasize what the trip might turn out like. Because we are open to every possibility and potentiality, we can approach our adventure with both excitement and optimism. In the real world, we often find ourselves overwhelmed by what seems to be an endless set of roadblocks lying between our goals and where we are currently. Yet when we are anticipating a new adventure, anything seems possible.

At this point in the action research process, you are in much the same position as a traveler who has just chosen a destination. In Chapter 2, where you identified potential research foci, you were, in effect, selecting the region you want to visit.

However, as any seasoned traveler knows, choosing a destination is just the beginning. The savvy traveler doesn't stop there. Part of the ritual, as well as the fun, of trip preparation is pouring over maps, reading guidebooks, and speaking with others who have traveled to the same or similar places. It is those activities that help the traveler to identify the cities, the sites, and the attractions he or she plans to visit and the experiences he or she hopes to have along the way. In Chapter 2, when you identified your priority achievement targets, you were identifying specific elements of your upcoming trip that you wanted to be sure not to miss.

VISUALIZING SUCCESS ■

As you daydreamed about your trip (through the reflective writing and reflective interviewing), you began visualizing what the perfect trip might look like. For the teacher conducting action research, this amounts to imagining what student, teaching, or program performance would be like if all the achievement targets were met in an excellent fashion.

Earlier it was said that achievement targets could be divided into performance, process, or program targets. If your focus is on a performance target, you should have started thinking of what you believe outstanding performance would be, if and when it is achieved. For example, if I decided to focus on improving student writing, I would be visualizing what a truly outstanding piece of expository writing would read like.

When researchers focus on process targets, they are trying to envision just how things might appear if the process or processes were working perfectly. For example, if I wanted to improve my ability to lead class discussions, I would try to visualize what my classroom would be like when productive and lively discussions were regularly taking place.

And when the focus is on a program target, the action researcher is envisioning all of the attributes of a truly outstanding program. For example, if we wanted to create a positive school climate, we would be asking ourselves what we would observe in a school where the climate was maximally supportive of child development.

Why Is Having a Clear Vision So Necessary?

It has been said, "If you don't know where you're going, any road will do." That is more than a clever play on words. When people are unsure of their destinations, they tend to take wrong turns, extend their trips with detours, and possibly end up where they hadn't wanted to go. In our classrooms, this could mean using inappropriate strategies, going off on tangents, and coming to the end of the year without our students possessing all the skills we had hoped and intended. Nothing feels worse for a classroom teacher. We feel a sense of loss. This is because at school, time always marches on. Opportunities don't often exist for going back and trying again (although in this era of high stakes, students are increasingly being required to go back and do it again—often at significant cost of their time, energy and self-esteem). This very real risk of losing our way and never getting to the desired place should motivate us to do the best possible planning for our action research, our planned exploration of a not-yet-visited destination.

Dedicated teachers don't need to be encouraged to plan. In fact, it is insulting to infer that teachers don't consistently engage in meaningful planning. When our students aren't performing at the level we want (meaning producing universally excellent work), it doesn't mean we didn't plan, nor does it mean we didn't follow our plans. In all likelihood, our plans were grounded in the best information we had available, and we implemented them with all the energy and enthusiasm we could muster. Simply beseeching us to plan "more" or "better" is like trying to get blood from a turnip. If we are already doing the best we know how and we are working at it as hard as we can, then what we are currently getting is likely the best we can expect—at least, without changing our approach.

■ DOING AN INSTRUCTIONAL POSTMORTEM

Let's return to the phrase, "If you don't know where you're going, any road will do," and think of a lesson, unit, or class you recently taught. Now cast yourself in a new role. You have now become your own personal teaching coach.

After a performance or a match, coaches often conduct postmortems on the recently completed action. They review everything that occurred, trying to learn as much as they can from their mistakes so they can avoid repeating them the next time. Now conduct an *instructional postmortem* on the class you just taught, in your role as teaching coach. Begin with an examination of the outcomes obtained, how your students ended up after instruction or, in the case of process or program targets, where you and/or your program ended up. For an athletic coach, this is the equivalent of the final score.

Following the travel metaphor, the first question the teaching coach should ask is,

What roads did you travel on your way to where you are now?

This is a critical question since it is logical to assume that if the same road is taken again, it will lead to the same destination. If we want to arrive at a different and better place, it will be necessary to take a different route. The instructional postmortem is a strategy that helps us learn from past experience and avoid repeating past mistakes.

A golfer trying to understand what led to his final score will mentally replay every hole, trying to recall each and every shot. When I do this in my role as my teaching coach, I review every lesson I taught and assignment made. I begin by thinking of a particular student whose final performance I wish to understand. Most often, I find myself considering a student whose final score disappointed me. Consequently, when I go over each activity engaged in by this student, I am not thinking of what I had hoped would happen (hit the green with my second shot and two putt) but what actually occurred (hit three balls into the woods, landed in the sand trap, and later four putted). The Instructional Post-Mortem Form (Figure 3.1) is designed to help you review a student's experience with a recently taught unit of instruction.

Once having reviewed the road we and our students traveled en route getting to our current destination, our next step is comparing our experience with that of others.

COMPARING YOUR EXPERIENCE ■
WITH THE EXPERIENCE OF OTHERS

Suppose you have spent the last 3 years saving for a European vacation. This could be a once-in-a-lifetime experience. You have arranged to spend as much time in Europe as possible, but alas, the time available is far less than you had hoped. Considering the expense involved as well as your time constraints, you are motivated to do whatever planning is necessary to provide the best possible travel experience.

You have good reason to want to minimize mistakes, such as wasting time at attractions with little to offer, and to get the most out of each venue. Going into an adventure blindly might make sense—it could even make the trip more exciting—providing you had unlimited time and money. But given your parameters, you want to engage in serious and focused planning. For most of us, this begins with research. Experienced travelers seek the insights of others who have taken similar trips. They want to learn from the successes, what was enjoyed most, as well as from the mistakes, the places to avoid. When collecting this information, the wise traveler has good reason to take note of where the advice is coming from. When weighing the opinions of others, it is always essential to consider the source. This

Figure 3.1   Instructional Postmortem Form

Briefly describe the lesson or instruction unit:

_____

_____

_____

_____

_____

State the skill or outcome that you had expected students to gain from this instruction:

_____

_____

_____

_____

List the significant characteristics of a learner whose experience you will be tracing (e.g., English language learner, precocious, cooperative, disruptive, gifted, etc.):

_____

_____

_____

_____

Describe the performance of this student following instruction:

_____

_____

_____

_____

_____

_____

Using the table provided, list in sequence all the significant instructional activities and facilitation provided during this unit or lesson and what the learner produced (grades, scores, products) or what you recall the learner doing in response to the activity:

Date	Activity	Performance, Comment

Use additional space if necessary.

Copyright © 2005 Corwin Press. All rights reserved. Reprinted from _The Action Research Handbook: A Four-Step Process for Educators and School Teams_, by Richard Sagor. Thousand Oaks, CA: Corwin Press, www .corwinpress.com. Reproduction authorized only for the local school site that has purchased this book.

caution is absolutely critical for our work as teacher researchers because this ensures that we are factoring in the variable of context—those unique aspects of the setting: the characteristics of the students, the teacher, and the group. When it comes to making decisions that will guide teaching and learning, understanding the context is often the most important factor and the one most frequently over-looked. We know this intuitively, but when adopting programs, we often fail to take this into account.

Most salespeople and developers of commercially available materials operate as though specific teaching and learning contexts are irrelevant. They presume that what worked in one setting will work in any setting. While this may be good for marketing, this posture denies what everyone who has ever taught in a classroom has learned: No two students, no two teachers, and no two classes can ever be exactly alike.

Gathering Insights From Colleagues

There are two main places where travelers go for information prior to embarking on their journeys. If they know people who have recently made the trip, they often contact them and arrange to hear about their experience. Similarly in the case of your action research, if you know of teachers who have been having success in your focus area, you might well want to talk to them and hear about their experience. The eight questions in the Colleague Interview Guide (Figure 3.2) can be helpful when asking professional colleagues about their experiences in your focus area.

Many travelers also find it helpful to consult guidebooks written and published by reputable authorities. When doing so, they also need to consider the source. One way to do this is by paying attention to the publication date. This way, they make use of the most current information available. Ultimately these two sources of data are used to plan an itinerary. While it is reasonable to rely on intuition and personal passion when selecting the overall destination (the focus for either action research or travel), it is hard to deny the prudence of consulting with experts before locking into an expensive program or nonrefundable ticket.

For action researchers, the equivalent of consulting guidebooks is conducting reviews of the literature.

The Literature Review

While the phrase *literature review* is certainly clear and descriptive, it frequently carries negative connotations for teachers preparing to conduct action research. Every teacher has conducted searches of the literature. For many, this last occurred when completing the requirements for a college degree. While some of us may have found the library research stimulating, many others will remember the process as unpleasant and time consuming.

More than any other reason, it is the time involved that keeps us from making the trip to the library to conduct a literature review prior to teaching a new unit or introducing a new concept. This is understandable, but terribly unfortunate. To save time, we often find ourselves going where others have gone before, yet we do so without the benefit of their counsel. When we encounter problems that could have been avoided with just a little helpful advice, we realize we have wasted valuable time and energy.

Figure 3.2   Colleague Interview Guide

The following questions can help you assess the applicability of an instructional process or program. Prior to conducting the first interview, ask yourself Questions 1 through 4 regarding your school or classroom. At the start of the interview, share a summary of your answers with the person or persons being interviewed.

Date: _____

Program, site: _____

Person(s) interviewed: _____

_____

_____

Your Setting	Interviewee's Setting
1. Why are you interested in the use of this program or process?	1. Why did you develop or introduce this program or process?
2. In what ways, if any, are the learners who will be affected by this program different from a typical group of their age?	2. In what ways, if any, are the learners who have been involved with this program different from a typical group of their age?
3. What are the characteristics of the staff members who would be working with this program or process (e.g., certification, teaching assignment, other responsibilities)?	3. What are the characteristics of the staff members who have been working with this program or process (e.g., certification, teaching assignment, other responsibilities)?
4. What resources will be available to support the use of this program or process?	4. What resources are used to support the use of this program or process?

(Continued)

Figure 3.2 (Continued)

Your Setting	Interviewee's Setting
	5. What specific outcomes do you attribute to the use of this program or process?
	6. In your opinion, what other factors contributed to the achievement of those outcomes?
	7. What problems did you encounter when developing or introducing this program or process?
	8. What else do you think a teacher or a school should know before implementing this program or process?

Copyright © 2005 Corwin Press. All rights reserved. Reprinted from *The Action Research Handbook: A Four-Step Process for Educators and School Teams*, by Richard Sagor. Thousand Oaks, CA: Corwin Press, www .corwinpress.com. Reproduction authorized only for the local school site that has purchased this book.

I am reminded of a commercial for oil filters that aired several years ago. The company wanted to encourage consumers to invest a few dollars in their product and use it for routine maintenance. They sold this idea by contrasting the minor cost of an inexpensive oil filter with the far larger cost of a complete engine rebuild. The company slogan was, "You can pay me now or pay me later!" At this point you may be saying, "Enough already! I don't need to be lectured on the value of standing on others' shoulders, but I still don't have the time to conduct lit reviews."

Fortunately, the Internet has made examining the professional knowledge base far easier than many of us recall from college, and continuous advances in search engine technology are making it more efficient all the time. The Literature Review Planning Form (Figure 3.3) was designed to help you structure and organize a literature review using the Internet.

Figure 3.3   Literature Review Planning Form

Review the area you've selected as the focus for your action research and the achievement targets you hope to impact through your work. Then answer the following questions:

1. List all the achievement targets you hope to see impacted by your actions.

_____

_____

_____

_____

_____

_____

2. List every strategy you are aware of that educators have used in their efforts to improve performance on the achievement targets listed.

_____

_____

_____

_____

_____

_____

3. Go over your answers to Questions 1 and 2, highlighting every key word.

4. Do an Internet search following these steps:
   a. Place the keywords in order of importance.
   b. Do a search using all of your key words.
   c. Repeat the search, dropping the least important key word.
   d. Repeat the process, dropping a key word each time, until you feel you have acquired enough information.
      Note: If you are unhappy with the results obtained, repeat the process using a different search engine.

5. Review the material from your search using the following table to record the strategies that have been reported as successful, noting the context and impact:

Strategy	Impact	Context (student and school)

6. Re-order the data from the table in order of the similarity of the reported context to your own:

Strategy	Impact

Copyright © 2005 Corwin Press. All rights reserved. Reprinted from *The Action Research Handbook: A Four-Step Process for Educators and School Teams,* by Richard Sagor. Thousand Oaks, CA: Corwin Press, www .corwinpress.com. Reproduction authorized only for the local school site that has purchased this book.

When using the Internet for research, it is especially important to consider the source. The best method I've found to do this is to follow these two steps:

1. Look in the article for the identity of a school or district that is currently using the approach. If it is said to be a promising practice but is not currently in use anywhere, this should raise a caution.

2. If an implementer is identified, contact teachers or others at the site by phone or e-mail who are currently implementing the program or have recently used it. Ask them about their experience, using the Colleague Interview Guide (Figure 3.2). When conducting your phone interview, pay particular attention to gleaning everything you can about what is unique about their context.

On occasion, after a literature review or an examination of commercially available materials, we identify a comprehensive program that appears to fit our needs. When this happens, we instinctively recognize that the most efficient thing to do is to *adopt and implement* the program as it was designed and packaged. This is another occasion where the travel metaphor may prove helpful.

Adopting Commercial Programs

Many times, vacationers will sign up for an all-inclusive package tour. This is a sensible thing to do, especially if they know other people who have taken and enjoyed that same tour and it includes their choice of venues. This is often the wisest, safest, and most economical strategy to follow. For me as an individual classroom teacher or for us as a faculty team, this is analogous to identifying an approach that other teachers in similar contexts have used with students similar to ours and obtained results that we would like to obtain. Adopting such an approach or program makes a great deal of sense.

The logic of this explains why adoption of commercially available programs is far and away the most widely used approach to educational program improvement. Finding what has worked for others in similar situations and then using it ourselves, prevents us from having to reinvent the wheel. But while the decision to purchase someone else's theory of action may be a wise initial course of action, it does not relieve us of the need to determine whether it turns out to be a good fit for us in our context through our own action research. In Chapter 4, we will discuss a process to use when conducting action research on adopted commercially available programs.

If after conducting a review of the pertinent literature, you haven't been able to identify ideas, programs, or strategies that you believe are superior to what you have been doing, it could mean that you will want to conduct a *descriptive* research study on your current program prior to introducing an innovation.

An investigation of what is occurring now may help you identify specific aspects of your program that could be modified to foster further improvement in performance on your priority achievement targets. Even so, you are encouraged to wait before deciding whether or not your research will be *quasi-experim*ental or *descriptive* until after completing Stage 2: Articulating Your Theory (see Chapters 4 and 5). Frequently, the activities engaged in as part of theory articulation will result in the generation of an innovative strategy that you will want to implement and investigate.

This is a good time to pause and review where we are with the action research process. By now you should have selected a focus area. You have visualized what excellence looks like and you have identified a set of critical subelements (priority achievement targets) that when taken together, should produce excellent performance in your focus area. Last, you have reviewed the literature and developed an understanding of the experience of others who have pursued improvement in the same focus area. This brings us to the last part of our work in Stage 1: establishing clear and unambiguous criteria for use in determining if you are, in fact, producing improvements with your achievement targets.

DEVELOPING CRITERIA TO MEASURE ■
CHANGES WITH PRIORITY ACHIEVEMENT TARGETS

Earlier you identified areas of student or program performance, called priority achievement targets. The targets spelled out specifically what you hoped to see improved. Once again it is worth emphasizing how wide the range of achievement targets can be. It was also stated that achievement targets could be divided into three categories: performance, process, and program. Those three categories cover a great deal of territory. Examples of the types of foci that come under each of these categories are listed in the box that follows.

Performance targets can include foci such as

- Changes in student academic performance
  - Improved computation skills
  - Improved inferential comprehension
  - Expanded variety of voices in writing

- Changes in student behavior
  - Increased attention to high-quality finished products
  - Increased on-task behavior
  - Enhanced cooperation and collaboration

- Changes in student attitude/affect
  - Enthusiasm for learning
  - Appreciation of art
  - Willingness to engage in long-range planning

Process targets can include foci such as

- Changes we would like to see in our teaching skills and methods
  - Leading more invigorating discussions
  - Providing clearer explanations for complex topics
  - Providing timely feedback to students

- Changes in school procedures
  - Adult-student rapport
  - School rules
  - Parent involvement

(Continued)

(Continued)

Program targets include foci such as

- Changes in curriculum
  - Making the content more relevant for the students
  - Integrating concepts across disciplines
  - Incorporating more creative problem-solving opportunities

- Changes in offerings
  - Elective programs
  - Required classes and experiences
  - Cocurricular programs

Occasionally, teacher researchers feel they should restrict the focus of their inquiries to a limited and specific range of targets. That is unfortunate for a number of reasons. When we place arbitrary limits on the focus of our inquiries we risk working on issues, which could actually be relatively low on our professional priority list. When this happens our work may, in fact, produce positive changes, but nevertheless, we will be reluctant to voluntarily engage in action research in the future. This is a reasonable decision, since the time and energy consumed conducting the research was time that could have been invested in other pursuits that might have proven more personally and professionally satisfying.

When we limit our focus to low-priority objectives, it most often happens for one of two reasons. The first is because of a premise that educators should only be concerned with goals that are cognitive and academic—a stance reinforced by much contemporary political rhetoric. This is a misguided notion for several reasons. There isn't a parent or student who doesn't expect more from education than mere facts and isolated skills. Furthermore, that isn't why most of us went into teaching. If all we wanted to accomplish was the transmission of bits of information, we would have been better off becoming computer programmers, not teachers. As was mentioned earlier and cannot be emphasized enough, action researchers' foci should be in their areas of passion. For that reason, it is once again appropriate to pause and ask yourself,

> What matters so much to me that if I spend my time pursuing improvement on it, I will deem my time as being well spent?

If your answer includes such issues as student motivation, behavior, attitudes, or affective characteristics, then those are perfectly legitimate foci for your action research.

There is a second reason why action researchers occasionally avoid the pursuit of high-priority but nonacademic achievement targets: the concern that many nonacademic targets, even those with great transcendent value, cannot be effectively assessed. This is incorrect. Any target that can be articulated can be assessed and with a high degree of validity and reliability.

■ CREATING RATING SCALES

Every car comes equipped with a tool for measuring its progress. This instrument is called an odometer. The tool most frequently used by educational action researchers for monitoring their progress when pursuing long-term or complex achievement targets is the rating scale. In recent years, educators began using the term *rubric* as a synonym for the rating scale. Before we leave Stage 1, it's a good idea to develop rating scales to measure growth on each of your priority achievement targets.

A relatively easy approach for constructing rating scales is to follow these three sequential steps:

- Visualize excellence
- Identify traits
- Create continua

Step 1: Visualizing Excellence

At the start of this chapter, we discussed the importance of holding a clear vision of success. Now, as we are moving into the arena of measurement, it is a good time to return to that concept. For each of the achievement targets that you hope to improve upon through your work, you should ask yourself this question:

If performance on this target was as I'd like, what would it look like?

To illustrate, let's take the case of Dr. Hernandez, an elementary school principal who is interested in helping her school become a more collegial workplace, believing that this will have a positive influence on student performance. To help her faculty reach this goal, she wants to encourage collaborative planning.

Dr. Hernandez might summarize her vision as follows:

I want to see a collegial workplace that is supportive of continuous progress toward universal excellence in student performance. I envision a professional work environment that supports the needs of the faculty and produces high levels of staff morale.

I envision all of the teachers feeling part of a supportive faculty team, which is able to apply creative problem solving in an effective and timely fashion, whenever a student or program issue arises. As our collegiality increases, I see a tighter and tighter alignment of curriculum, instruction, and assessment.

For a classroom example, we'll consider Mr. Collins, a fourth-grade teacher who wants his students to become more proficient readers. He might describe his vision this way:

I want to see my students become skillful readers. It isn't enough for them to gain the skills to make use of grade-level material; I also want them to be able to read between the lines. I want them to understand more than just what the author is saying but also to gain insights into the author's point of view. I want them to appreciate the full versatility of the English language by being able to identify a variety of techniques authors employ to convey meaning and tone.

Both principal and teacher have expressed visions, which helped clarify their targets. The principal is working on a program target, the development of a more collegial school, while the teacher is in pursuit of a performance target, the creation of skillful readers.

Step 2: Identifying Traits

Frequently, significant targets such as these are made up of subelements (sub-skills) that I refer to as *traits*. A trait is a specific quality that is characteristic of a performance, process, or program that is succeeding in hitting the target.

In the case of the collegial school, one can identify the traits by carefully reading through the principal's vision. I noted the following traits as being characteristic of the school Dr. Hernandez envisioned:

Universal excellence in student performance

Excellent staff morale

A team culture

Staff as skilled problem solvers

Alignment of curriculum, instruction, and assessment

Mr. Collins' goal of producing more skillful readers also contained several subelements:

Ability to use grade-level material

Enjoyment of reading

Literal comprehension skills

Inferential comprehension skills

In Chapter 7, when our focus shifts to the design of a comprehensive data-collection plan, we examine how action researchers can make use of rating scales as instruments for data collection. However, at this point, our rating scales will serve two other specific and important functions:

1. Help us to further clarify the targets we are pursuing.

2. Provide us with confidence that we can effectively document changes in the level of performance on our targets.

Step 3: Creating Continua

Rating scales having an odd number of points are highly recommended for monitoring performance because it can be valuable to identify a clear midpoint. I operationally define the midpoint on rating scales as "good performance" or "meeting expectations." Good performance, right in the middle, is where I would like all my students to be; functionally, it can be understood to mean "at grade level."

Constructing the rating scale begins by listing the subelements (the traits) of the target on the column on the extreme left. Using the Rating Scale Worksheet (see Figure 3.4), list one trait per row. In the middle column, write your definition of what constitutes *a good level of performance* for each trait, in bulleted form. Mr. Collins, who is working on improving his students' reading, might put these items in the middle column (#3) for the trait of inferential comprehension:

1. The student can correctly state the main idea.

2. The student can articulate the author's thesis and back up the thesis statement with multiple details from the text.

Figure 3.4   Rating Scale Worksheet

Trait	Emerging (1)	Basic (2)	Developing (3)	Proficient (4)	Fluent (5)

Copyright © 2005 Corwin Press. All rights reserved. Reprinted from *The Action Research Handbook: A Four-Step Process for Educators and School Teams,* by Richard Sagor. Thousand Oaks, CA: Corwin Press, www.corwinpress.com. Reproduction authorized only for the local school site that has purchased this book.

Then ask, *What would be the minimum performance* one might observe that could still be called a demonstration of the trait? This is a level of performance that constitutes the smallest movement in the right direction, the tiniest baby step along the road to proficiency. For inferential comprehension, this could be something like, "being capable of making a reasoned guess at the author's main idea." In the column labeled *Basic*, to the left of the middle column, write down the observable behaviors that you feel constitute the minimum performance observable on each trait.

Last, ask what *a truly outstanding example of performance* on this trait would look like. Here you are envisioning near perfection in performance. For inferential comprehension, Mr. Collins might list the following items:

1. The student can accurately retell and support the author's thesis with multiple details from the text.

2. The student can draw logical inferences about the author's point of view.

3. The student can persuasively support those inferences by referencing specific rhetorical techniques, language usage, and vocabulary employed by the author.

Figure 3.5 reflects Mr. Collins' rating scale partially filled in for the trait of inferential comprehension. Now, using the rating scale worksheet provided (Figure 3.4), build a five-point rating scale that you believe illustrates a continuum of performance for each priority achievement target.

> The more long-term the achievement target, the more columns you may need on your rating scale. However, be sure that the distinctions between the performances that make up each step on the rating scale are clear, distinct from each other, and unambiguous.

■ THE SPECIAL PROBLEM OF LONG-RANGE GOALS

Both of the targets discussed in the previous section—building a collegial faculty and developing skillful readers—are significant goals. In all likelihood, it will take considerable time to move performance to the top of the scale. Nevertheless, it is reasonable for a fourth-grade teacher or a principal to expect improvement on the target during the course of his or her initial research.

There are targets, be they academic or nonacademic, that educational action researchers often shy away from simply because they take so long to complete. The long-term nature of these targets makes them appear nearly impossible to monitor. For example, it is common for educators to value priority targets for their students such as

- Becoming lifelong learners
- Preparing for success in college
- Possessing the character trait of integrity

However, because it takes many years of concentrated effort to get students to success on these targets, many action researchers elect to avoid them. That is

Figure 3.5 Rating Scale Reading Proficiency

Trait	Emerging (1)	Basic (2)	Developing (3)	Proficient (4)	Fluent (5)
1. Ability to read grade-level material					
2. Enjoyment of reading					
3. Literal compre-hension					
4. Inferential compre-hension	After reading a grade-level-appropriate essay, the student can accurately restate the main idea.	After reading a grade-level-appropriate essay, the student can accurately retell the author's thesis.	After reading a grade-level-appropriate essay, the student can accurately retell and support the author's thesis with multiple details from the text.	After reading a grade-level-appropriate essay, the student can accurately retell and support the author's thesis with multiple details from the text and can draw logical inferences about the author's point of view.	After reading a grade-level-appropriate essay, the student can accurately retell and support the author's thesis with multiple details from the text, can draw logical inferences about the author's point of view, and can persuasively support those inferences by referencing specific rhetorical techniques, language usage, and vocabulary used by the author.

SOURCE: Adapted from Sagor (2000).

unfortunate because, in this era of high-stakes testing, if we don't focus on something and measure progress toward its attainment, it is unlikely to get the attention it deserves.

To understand the challenge of assessing progress on long-term targets, I use the work of the U.S. Space Agency, NASA, as an analogy. As part of its interplanetary studies, NASA has sent several Cassini probes to make fly-bys of Saturn and Jupiter and relay data on those planets back to Earth.

These are long-range projects in two ways. First, it took years to develop the technologies needed to design spacecraft capable of performing these missions. Furthermore, once the probes are launched, it takes several years to reach Saturn and Jupiter. Clearly it would have been folly for NASA to bypass these projects simply because they were so long-term. After all, interplanetary studies are at the very core of its mission. But it would be equally wrong for it to proceed with such ambitious projects without a strategy to continuously monitor progress.

Consequently, the two key assessment questions for NASA became

- How do we determine if our research and development efforts are proceeding on schedule?
- Once a spacecraft has been launched, how can we determine if the spacecraft is on course to pass by Saturn and Jupiter as scheduled, several years hence?

The issues those questions present for rocket scientists (aerospace action researchers) are not conceptually different than the ones confronting educational action researchers pursuing long-term learning goals. Keep in mind, it could be 25 years before anyone will know with certainty if any particular student has, in fact, become a lifelong learner. Likewise, character traits are not acquired overnight. The challenge for NASA and the educator is one and the same: creating systems that reliably assess incremental advances on targets that may not be fully realized for years to come.

■ ASSESSING RATE OF GROWTH

It usually isn't enough to simply know that progress is being made. Steady progress could be occurring but at such slow rates as to be declared ineffective. Consequently, when working with long-range goals, the question that needs asking concerns whether the rate of progress is satisfactory. When it comes to the achievement of academic objectives, most educators are familiar with the concept of *rate of growth*. In the common school vernacular, when a student continues to perform *at grade level*, we classify his or her rate of growth as appropriate. This translates as achieving *one year's growth in one year's time*.

When working on a 5-year project, the appropriate rate of growth is progress at a rate that will result in completion of the project in 60 months' time. For every NASA mission, there is an expectation of when the launch should occur. Therefore, the acceptable rate of progress is one that will have everything ready to go and in place on or before the projected launch date.

Recent federal regulations in the United States have codified an acceptable rate of growth for students. The No Child Left Behind Act (2002) requires schools to demonstrate that individual students, groups of students, and entire student bodies achieve "adequate yearly progress" (AYP). The procedures for accomplishing this involve the use of annually administered tests designed to determine if the progress made by the students during the past year was at a rate sufficient to get them to the targets on time. This monitoring system, even when accurate, is far from comforting for classroom teachers. It will be too late to make instructional modifications for that student if teachers have to wait for the results of the annual spring testing. It is like receiving feedback on the efficacy of a 365-day weight loss program by weighing yourself only at the end of the year.

DETERMINING ADEQUATE ■
YEARLY PROGRESS IN REAL TIME

Let's assume I am a teacher who is deeply committed to helping each of my students make adequate yearly progress. And let's assume I have developed a very clear vision regarding the target performance that I am after. In most cases, this would be the skills that the testing program assumes my students will possess by the end of the year. Last, we'll assume I am unwilling to wait until June to determine if my hypothesis on the best way to prepare them is working as I had hoped (helping them progress at a rate of "one year's growth in one year's time").

In all likelihood, the type of rating scale discussed earlier in this chapter won't be satisfactory. As good as a 5-, 7-, or 9-point rating scale may be, it's not likely to be sensitive enough to detect minor incremental developments. Using such a scale would be like assessing my weight reduction program by weighing myself every morning, but doing so with an industrial scale that reports weight in 20-pound increments. While it might be a great scale, it can't provide me with feedback that is sensitive or precise enough to meet my needs.

Figure 3.6 is a visual from NASA that illustrates the trajectory of a Cassini spacecraft as it completes its 7-year mission. By knowing the launch date and the current position of the spacecraft, researchers can use this diagram at any point during the mission to determine if the vehicle is, in fact, proceeding appropriately—achieving its AYP.

Let's now look at an academic example (see Figure 3.7). In this case, we will assume the goal is to have our students prepared to successfully enter advanced placement calculus when they finish 11th grade. Let's also assume that at least some students entering kindergarten in our district aren't yet able to identify numerals correctly. Figure 3.7 illustrates the slope of the growth that needs to be demonstrated by a student entering school with zero math knowledge while staying on track to meet the goal of succeeding with AP calculus as a senior.

As teachers, what we need is to monitor our students' rates of growth by plotting their performance as they move up the grades. A quick look at a longitudinal graph will tell us if the slope of progress reflects a rate of growth that is

1. Right on target (at AYP), enabling the student to take calculus as a senior

2. Faster than expected and would enable the student to take calculus earlier (faster than AYP)

3. Below the expectation (slower than AYP), not ready for calculus as a senior

Figure 3.8 indicates the rate of progress of two students; one who is performing at a rate faster than AYP and one at a slower rate than AYP.

Figure 3.6 Cassini Interplanetary Trajectory

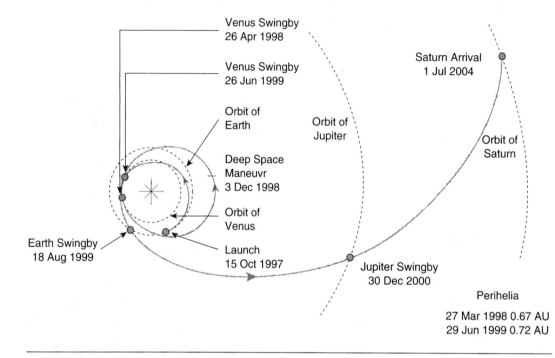

SOURCE: http://saturn.jpl.nasa.gov/cgibin/gs2.cgi

Figure 3.7 Rate-of-Growth Expectations

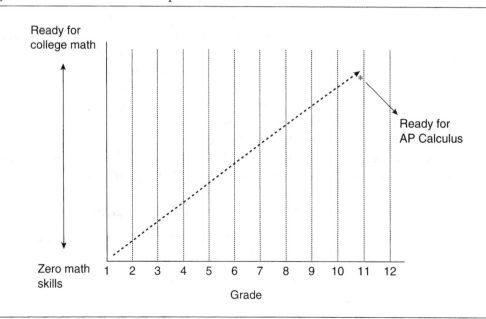

Figure 3.8 Rate-of-Growth Expectations: Two Students

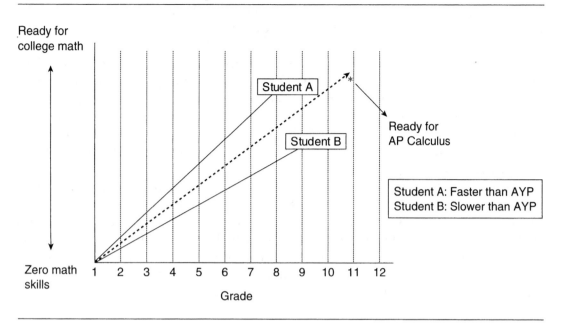

PRODUCING YOUR OWN ■
RATE-OF-GROWTH CHARTS

There are five steps you can follow to produce a rate-of-growth chart that can be used to track progress toward a long-term target. By using such a device, you can meaningfully trace the efficacy of your work on a target, even when ultimate proficiency cannot be determined for several years to come.

Step 1: When pursuing a long-range, multiyear target, the first step is to place in sequence a list of the skills, backed up by an example of the type of work that is expected of students on entrance into each grade, for this particular achievement target.

Step 2: Then examine the list to determine if it is logical, has any obvious gaps, and seems achievable. (Space won't permit going any deeper into this issue in this text, but this is an absolutely critical aspect of the curriculum development work that needs to occur if a school is to effectively monitor its efforts to comply with the No Child Left Behind Act [2002].)

Step 3: Now take a look at the examples of on-target work for a student entering the grade you will be teaching and for a student exiting your grade. Ask yourself or your team to brainstorm every single little baby step of a skill or proficiency that lies between the entry piece of work and the exit piece. Come up with as many miniskills as possible.

Step 4: Make any adjustments to the sequence of the skills on your list so it's as accurate and inclusive as possible. It's okay if the subskills on the list aren't sequential in nature, but to the best degree possible, place them in order.

Step 5: Now divide the list by the number of weeks in the school year (usually 36). Let's assume that you identified 72 separate subskills. If a student is acquiring skills at the rate of two per week, he or she is making AYP.

Step 6: (Note: This step can only be done on a schoolwide or systemwide basis.) Place the listings of subskills on a continuum across all the grades served in your school. Then conduct an entry assessment for each child, either at the beginning of the school year or when he or she enters your room. Make plans to conduct an exit assessment of each student as well. With this type of assessment, you will be able to determine the rate of progress for each of the children during the time each of them spent in your class.

Keep in mind that what is AYP for any student is a value judgment. If I were teaching remedial students and I held high aspirations for each one of them, my goal might be to produce a rate of growth in excess of one year's growth in one year's time, since that would be required if they were to catch up with their peers. But, regardless of how AYP is defined, a rate-of-growth chart will enable you to monitor and adjust in a timely fashion without having to wait for the year-end test or perhaps several years, if you are looking for evidence of achievement of a long-term goal.

■ END OF STAGE 1

We have now finished our exploration of the first stage of the action research process, clarifying the vision and targets. To recap, at this point you have selected a focus for your research that relates to an area

- That you care deeply about
- Where performance could be improved
- Where the actions needed to make changes in performance are within your sphere of authority

In addition, you have identified a set of specific priority achievement targets where you hope to see demonstrable improvement. By now you should have consulted the literature and considered the experience of others who have worked at achieving success in the same focus area. Last, after reflecting on each of the traits or subelements of your target, you have identified a range of observable performance and a pace of development that you feel constitutes AYP.

You have now teased out and achieved some degree of precision on where you want to go and how you could measure your progress as you travel to the desired destination. You have closed your eyes and seen the Promised Land as well as the mileposts you expect to pass along the way.

This brings us to the threshold of Stage 2: Articulating a Theory of Action. This is where you will engage in the rigorous but fun work of figuring out what route has the greatest potential for getting you closer to your vision.

4

Articulating a Theory in Action

n Stage 1 we identified priority achievement targets and examined what would constitute appropriate growth on those targets. This brings us to the second stage of the action research process, articulating a theory of action. When becoming action researchers, action becomes more than just our first name. Our concern about providing the very best professional *action* is the only sensible reason for engaging in this work. The work up until now has been very important; in fact, the work you did in Stage 1 was essential to your ultimate success. But it is here at Stage 2 that the creative intellectual work begins: It is in the work of theory development that you will be designing original strategies and techniques with real promise for producing better results than have ever been produced in the past.

Action research, often referred to by other terms, is a key aspect of the systems approach to continuous improvement pioneered by W. Edwards Deming (1986/2000). Deming asserts that 95% of organizational performance is attributable to the tactics, strategies and processes used. Increasingly, research has shown that organizational success is not the result of the inherent goodness or badness of the personnel working in the organization. Performance is not a factor of *who* is doing the work but rather, how things are being done (Deming, 1986/2000; Senge, 1990). Consequently, when there is an improvement in performance, the credit belongs to the theory of action that was developed and followed. So if we find ourselves disappointed in performance, it doesn't mean we are bad people or less than competent professionals. It indicates that our actions and the theories behind them weren't adequate to the challenge we faced, and consequently those actions need to be changed.

Action research is an empowering strategy. Exercising control over the prevailing operative theory of action is the most powerful thing a professional can do. But the idea of taking responsibility for critiquing our own practices and designing innovative solutions, while at the heart of this process, generates some controversy. The two criticisms most often voiced against empowering teachers with this authority are the following:

1. Educators aren't capable of attending to theory and program design while meeting their other responsibilities.

2. An adequate professional knowledge base already exists, and educators ought to be simply and faithfully implementing those practices in their classrooms.

■ IF NOT US, WHO?

The first argument, that practicing educators aren't the ones who should be doing this work, flies in the face of the reality that teachers face on a daily basis. All professional work is complex. And teaching is arguably the most complex, with hundreds of variables influencing each practitioner decision (see the discussion in Chapter 1). Due to the complexity involved in professional decision making, the development and maintenance of each profession's knowledge base has always been considered part of the job of the profession itself. Furthermore, in other professions, the people who must take the action are expected to design the innovations, conduct the research, and consequently produce the body of professional knowledge. This makes sense. After all, who else is in a position to identify the problems, understand the context, and integrate new insights into prevailing routines than those working on the front lines?

I have two dogs that I love dearly. Every time I take one of my golden retrievers to the vet, I am literally betting their lives on the treatment protocol that the veterinarian chooses to administer. I find it comforting to know that it was veterinarians who conducted the research that informs the practice of the people who work with my dogs on a regular basis.

When tasks are simple and straightforward, it is more efficient to have someone other than the line worker responsible for designing and approving the practices to be used. This is why supervisors are hired to direct blue-collar work. But when the work is complex, when it requires an understanding of nuance and idiosyncratic behavior and calls for constant assessment by a trained eye as well as continual adjustments in the operative theories of action, it must be informed by the insights of those taking the action: the practitioners themselves.

■ AN ADEQUATE KNOWLEDGE BASE ALREADY EXISTS

The second criticism leveled at teacher research is a bit bizarre. The stated goal of educational policy throughout most of North America is getting every student to high levels of performance on meaningful goals. If a knowledge base exists that documents how to accomplish this, why is this research so widely ignored? Personally, I know of no evidence that reports that any city, state, or country has ever succeeded in getting all of its children to high levels of performance on meaningful objectives. So unless there has been a worldwide and intergenerational conspiracy to deny the children of the world access to a good education, it would appear that the answers on how to accomplish universal student success have eluded the best and brightest throughout history. It is safe to say that the current educational knowledge base is inadequate to get us to the expected levels of performance.

So, in the words of the Hebrew sage, Hillel,

> If not us, who?
> If not here, where?
> If not now, when?

GOING BEYOND PROVEN PRACTICES: ■
BUILDING A THEORY OF ACTION

In Chapter 3's discussion of the literature review, the careful reader might have noticed that I avoided a phrase that has become part of the current school improvement vernacular: *proven practice*. It is a term that rolls nicely and easily off the tongue. The word *proven* delivers a good public relations punch, but shopping for and adopting proven practices is a strategy for school improvement that doesn't work as well as its name suggests.

Obviously, there is nothing wrong with making use of successful strategies. When a practice has been proven to work in a context similar to yours and the results that it was proven to produce meet your standards, then adopting that practice for your school or classroom makes absolute sense.

External Pressure and Proven Practices

In a desire to encourage educators to make use of the best available practices, many government agencies and publicly supported programs now mandate the use of what are called scientifically proven practices. On the surface, policies like these seem quite rational. After all, if a strategy has been scientifically proven to be effective, it ought to be employed whenever and wherever appropriate. To ignore a proven practice would constitute educational malpractice, since it would mean denying a student a beneficial educational experience. In other aspects of our lives, it is easy to think of proven practices that it is wise to follow. For example,

- File your taxes by April 15th or you will be penalized.
- When arguing a case, show respect for the presiding judge or there will be unwelcome consequences.
- Avoid contact with other people when you have a contagious disease.

Failing to adopt these proven practices would be irresponsible. It puts you or others at risk.

But what of the so-called proven practices in teaching and learning? Repeatedly we hear of programs that were proven to be successful. Furthermore, when we examine data on these programs, we might encounter impressive statistics, such as

- With this program, attendance improved for 80% of the students.
- While using this program, 75% of the students posted gains in comprehension.

It is only right that we are impressed with gains like those. But simply adopting and faithfully implementing programs with such results won't prove satisfying for most educators in the long run. This is because in the opinion of most dedicated teachers, a 75% to 80% success rate isn't adequate. While at first blush those statistics might sound impressive, stated in another way, the same data says the following:

- Attendance showed no improvement for 20% of the students.
- While using this program, 1 out of 4 students showed no improvement in comprehension.

If an adopted program can be expected to work as well for others as it did where it was proven successful, then the teacher or faculty adopting these programs should expect to leave their classroom every day knowing that 20% to 25% of the students won't be prospering. Few dedicated teachers will find this a very inviting prospect. Simply adopting a program that hasn't produced universal student success and then considering your program development work as complete means accepting a degree of failure as inevitable. Having to go along with such an assumption is both emotionally and morally untenable for most teachers.

This is not an argument against using practices that have worked with many students. However, it does alert us to a set of critical questions that should be raised whenever a review of research or school policy leads us toward implementing a proven practice.

The first question is, *Who has this been proven to work with?* As professionals concerned with promoting universal student success, we need to know about the characteristics of the group who prospered as well as those who didn't. Were there patterns that could help us predict success or failure for some of our students? For example, did boys and girls succeed with in the past, or fail in equal proportions? Was this program successful with gifted students? How about kids with dyslexia?

If a proposed or adopted program appears to be beneficial for your students, then by all means, you ought to use it. However if there is a type of student for whom the program has not succeeded with in the past, and you have similar students in your classes, then you have found an excellent focus for your action research. Such a finding might cause you to want to investigate

> What *alterations, modifications,* or *alternatives* to this program would make it more likely that additional students will succeed, especially with the types of students that hadn't experienced success with the program elsewhere?

This question highlights the challenge for any inquiring educator who is continually trying to isolate techniques that promise to increase the percentage of students experiencing success. There is no escaping the truth of the saying, *"If we keep doing what we've been doing, we will keep getting what we've been getting."*

Even if we were willing to accept the status quo as good enough, doing so is now a violation of U.S. education policy. The No Child Left Behind Act (2002) mandates that students in every identifiable subcategory in each school must be making AYP on their state's priority achievement targets. Just obtaining the same degree of success achieved the previous year will no longer be enough. Now students in every cohort need to do better than their predecessors did.

Since continuing to get what we've been getting won't satisfy our own high expectations and it is guaranteed to put us outside compliance with government regulations, we have no choice but to turn that old saying around and state it in reverse:

If we want to get *more than* we've been getting, then we need to figure out how to *do things differently* than we've being doing.

While this doesn't mean you will forever be engaged in conducting full-blown action research projects, it does mean you will probably be involved with the four stages of the action research process in some way—*envisioning success, clarifying a theory to get there, collecting data while trying it out, and reflecting on results*—for as long as you are teaching.

One of the benefits of using the best practices developed by others is that it helps put boundaries on our inquiries. When we are building a revised theory of action on top of an existing theory of action (that has already succeeded with a significant number of students), we aren't trying to solve the entire riddle by ourselves and we aren't starting from scratch.

Whether we are building on a strong program that has been implemented elsewhere or creating our own program, being *innovative* in the development of a theory of action isn't a choice; it is essential. Since, by necessity, things will have to be done differently than they were before, creativity will be needed to figure out what ought to be changed. If the theory of action we develop is to succeed, it will need to take into account three factors:

- What is known about the context where it will be implemented?
- What is contained in the professional knowledge base?
- What have we come to understand through the wisdom of practice, our own experience?

TWO KINDS OF VARIABLES   ■

In Chapter 3, you established criteria via a rating scale for measuring changes in performance on your priority achievement target. The term researchers use for a phenomenon they are trying to improve or change is their *dependent variable*. The word *dependent* is used because the researcher is positing that changes in performance are dependent on something happening. For example, if I desire to lose weight, my achievement target is how much I hope to weigh. The criteria I would establish to determine change on this target would be my weight in pounds and ounces as measured by my bathroom scale. Since I believe that changes in behavior and diet can have an impact on how much I weigh, my weight is the dependent variable in my search for a lighter me.

Another type of variable refers to the phenomena that researchers posit will influence changes in the dependent variable. This is called the *independent variable*. The term *independent* is used because the experimenters are free to adjust the independent variables however they think best. Later they will determine if those adjustments were worthwhile by looking for corresponding changes in measurements of the dependent variable. The independent variables that I might choose to adjust, in my investigation of weight loss, are my behaviors (what I eat and what exercise I engage in). This relationship is illustrated in the following table.

Choice of Independent Variables = $\longrightarrow$ *Change* in the Dependent Variable
(our actions) (achievement target)

The rating scales you developed will be used in your action research to measure changes in the dependent variable, your achievement target. From this point on, we will use the terms *achievement target* and *dependent variable* as synonyms. So far, we have been concentrating on the dependent variables, your priority achievement targets. Now it is time to begin the process of identifying the independent variables that you believe have the greatest potential for producing the desired changes in the dependent variable.

■ CREATING MILEPOSTS ON THE ROUTE TO MASTERY

As we worked our way through Stage 1, we broke down our large visions into parts. We moved from a general improvement focus to a comprehensive vision of success on specific achievement targets. Then we broke down the achievement targets into sub-elements (traits) that could be effectively assessed. As we develop a theory of action, we will engage in the same process but in reverse order. In constructing a theory of action, we build a comprehensive theory by starting with the constituent parts and then building up to the big picture.

Discerning the subelements of our target (the traits) was important because performance on the target could be defined as the sum of performance on the constituent traits. Likewise, when we have completed our theory of action, we will see that the efficacy of the larger theory is the sum of a set of particular actions, the independent variables.

■ INFERRING INDEPENDENT VARIABLES

The first step in the process of building our theory is to integrate what we already understand from personal experience with what we've gathered from the review of the literature. We begin by creating a list of all the key factors (independent variables) we think ought to be addressed through our actions if significant improvement is to occur on the achievement targets.

Let's put ourselves in the position of Dr. Hernandez, the elementary principal who was hoping to increase the problem-solving capacity of her faculty. Reflecting on the key variables that she as principal could influence, she might have generated the following list:

- Provide adequate time for teachers to meet.
- Provide easy access to pertinent data on student performance.
- Clarify and keep a faculty focus on priority school goals.
- Be personally engaged with each faculty work group.

Identifying these critical independent variables was important, but it didn't provide her with enough direction on what specific actions she could or should take to achieve the desired results. In addition, the list wasn't prioritized nor did it provide any insight into how these separate actions might influence each other. Consequently, she would have a hard time articulating a reasoned and coherent strategy for hitting her target without thinking through the answers to two additional questions:

- What is the relative importance of these identified variables?
- What are the relationships and interactions between them?

In this and the next chapter, we examine two strategies that, when taken together, can help action researchers address both of those questions. The first is a technique called the *priority pie.*

USING THE PRIORITY PIE TO IDENTIFY, ■
CLARIFY, AND WEIGH INDEPENDENT VARIABLES

Twenty-five years of educational research have clearly established the relationship between time and learning. Both the allocation of time and the time spent on-task have been shown to be key correlates of learning. Time is, without a doubt, the most valuable resource under our control. And since class time is a zero-sum commodity, the decisions we make on how to spend this scarce resource are crucial. It isn't an overstatement to assert that in large measure, our effectiveness in hitting our targets is determined by the wisdom of our choices regarding the expenditure of the time available to us. The priority pie is a simple strategy, one that will help you determine how you might most effectively allocate this critical resource.

To demonstrate the use of the *priority pie* strategy, let's follow two hypothetical action researchers as they work their way through the theory-building process. One is Dr. Hernandez, trying to enhance the problem-solving capacity of her faculty. Her target, changing the organizational approach to professional problem solving at her school, could be classified as a program target. The second project is the work of Mr. Seeker, a middle school English teacher; he wants to increase his students' success on an academic performance target: He wants his eighth-grade students to develop the ability to write unified, sequential, and persuasive five-paragraph essays.

The priority pie process that they will be using has four steps:

- Brainstorming
- Summarizing
- Evaluating
- Graphing

Step 1: Brainstorming the Critical Independent Variables

If we are to succeed in improving performance on our priority achievement targets, we need to identify and attend to *each key independent variable.* The process of identification must occur consciously and deliberately because, should an essential variable be overlooked, our ultimate success will be affected. Therefore, the first step is thinking through and answering the following question:

What are the issues, factors, programs, and processes that *must* be addressed to achieve success with this target (to have all participants performing at or above grade-level expectations)?

We've already seen Dr. Hernandez's four items. Mr. Seeker responded with this list:

I need to provide both *instruction* and *feedback* for my students on the following items:
- Organization skills
- Persuasive voice
- Editing skills
- Vocabulary
- Grammar and mechanics

Step 2: Summarizing the Independent Variables

Once action researchers feel confident that they have identified the key independent variables, they can begin to articulate an emergent theory of action. At this stage, Dr. Hernandez could articulate her theory as follows:

> For the faculty to succeed in becoming an effective problem-solving team, I need to ensure that adequate time is provided for teachers to meet and work collaboratively. I also need to make sure that they have access to all the pertinent data and information needed to make successful decisions. Since a sense of common purpose is essential, I need to take steps to achieve clarity on our school goals and work at keeping our collective attention focused on schoolwide priorities. To build support for this process, I need to find a way to become a partner with each faculty work group while they are addressing school goals.

Mr. Seeker might summarize his emerging theory this way:

> For my students to produce proficient, persuasive five-paragraph essays, they will need direct instruction and feedback from me. I need to teach them how to develop their organizational skills, editing skills, word choice skills, skills in the use of mechanics and grammar, as well as the development of a persuasive voice. And I need to provide feedback on their work in each of these areas.

Since time and energy are limited, both of these action researchers realize they need to apportion the finite time they have available among each of the competing actions (independent variables) mentioned in their emergent theories. This brings them to Step 3.

Step 3: Conducting an Intuitive Regression Analysis

The next step in the priority pie process is determining the amount of emphasis that should be invested in each identified factor. Determining the relative importance of each item on the list is a judgment call, one that you will ultimately have to make for yourself. It is an informed judgment based on a combination of your review of the literature and your own past experience.

You can accomplish this by dividing your time and energy across the list of items, based on the perceived importance of each item to the realization of the whole, excellent performance on the target. This can be done using the Intuitive Regression Analysis Worksheet, seen in Figure 4.1. Each item brainstormed in Step 1 is assigned a percentage reflecting how critical you believe that item is to the achievement of the whole. There is no limit to the percentage that can be assigned to any one item; however, the total cannot exceed 100%.

Step 4: Graphically Displaying the Emerging Theory

Once you have completed your analysis using the Intuitive Regression Analysis Worksheet, your emergent theory can be drawn as a pie graph, and a summary paragraph should be written that explains your assumptions on the appropriate allocation of resources. Figures 4.2 and 4.3 show Dr. Hernandez's and Mr. Seeker's narratives and graphs, respectively.

Figure 4.1 Intuitive Regression Analysis

Using the following form, make a judgment regarding the relative importance of each of the factors you identified as critical to success on this achievement target. Use a separate form for each target you are pursuing.

Achievement Target: _____

List Each Factor Deemed Critical to Fostering Success With This Achievement Target	Importance of This Factor (%)
Total:	100%

Copyright © 2005 Corwin Press. All rights reserved. Reprinted from *The Action Research Handbook: A Four-Step Process for Educators and School Teams,* by Richard Sagor. Thousand Oaks, CA: Corwin Press, www .corwinpress.com. Reproduction authorized only for the local school site that has purchased this book.

The development of a priority pie is an extremely important part of our work in Stage 2. It forces us to do the hard intellectual work of determining what we believe is of importance, and it also causes us to reflect on the relative importance of each aspect of the work. As important as this is, it still lacks the detail and precision necessary to give adequate direction to our work. There are still several other crucial things that still need to be considered before we can declare our theory of action to be complete and go about implementing it. Even the best priority pie won't provide enough clarity and direction to proceed to the action phase. If we want to have confidence that the "theory" we will be following has a high likelihood of producing success, we first need to know and incorporate the following:

- What specific actions need to be taken to satisfy each slice of the priority pie?
- Who is involved in each of these actions?
- When should those actions occur?
- Will multiple actions need to occur simultaneously?
- Is there a sequence of events that should be followed?
- If problems are encountered, what types of remedial steps should be taken?

Figure 4.2   Enhancing Problem-Solving Capacity

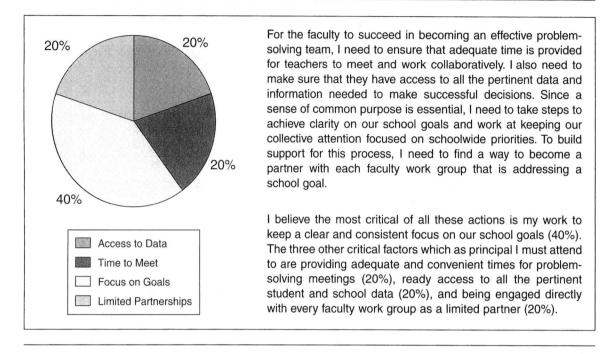

For the faculty to succeed in becoming an effective problem-solving team, I need to ensure that adequate time is provided for teachers to meet and work collaboratively. I also need to make sure that they have access to all the pertinent data and information needed to make successful decisions. Since a sense of common purpose is essential, I need to take steps to achieve clarity on our school goals and work at keeping our collective attention focused on schoolwide priorities. To build support for this process, I need to find a way to become a partner with each faculty work group that is addressing a school goal.

I believe the most critical of all these actions is my work to keep a clear and consistent focus on our school goals (40%). The three other critical factors which as principal I must attend to are providing adequate and convenient times for problem-solving meetings (20%), ready access to all the pertinent student and school data (20%), and being engaged directly with every faculty work group as a limited partner (20%).

Figure 4.3   Five-Paragraph Persuasive Essay

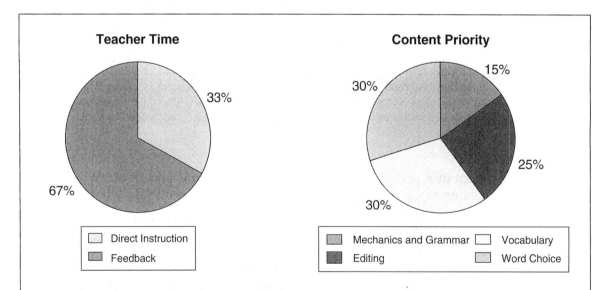

For my students to produce proficient, persuasive five-paragraph essays, they need ample direct instruction and feedback from me as they develop their organizational skills, editing skills, word choice skills, skills in the use of mechanics and grammar, and the development of a persuasive voice.

I feel the most critical of these skills is the development of voice and the related area of word choice and vocabulary. Together, these two elements account for 60% of what my students need to know. Mechanics and grammar skills amount to 15%, with editing skills being 25% of the equation. I believe that my students' success is dependent on my providing appropriate direct instruction and feedback. Since I believe that effective writing requires practice, I believe they need to spend 2/3 of their time and energy in the act of writing. For this reason, 67% of my work will be focused on providing students with feedback on their writing and 33% on direct skill instruction.

In experimental science and all other forms of exploration, it is necessary that the explorers start their work with as detailed a plan of action as possible. The process of clearly and unambiguously articulating one's plan of action serves several purposes:

- A detailed plan provides guidance and direction for the work.
- If and when success is achieved, the plan that was followed provides a road map that others can use as they attempt to reach the same destination.
- If the results don't come out as expected, the plan can be meticulously retraced to find out where problems were encountered.

USING THE PRIORITY PIE WITH DESCRIPTIVE RESEARCH   ■

When conducting *descriptive* action research, it is equally important to have clarity on the theories of action that are being observed and documented. The essential difference is that with descriptive research, the purpose is to clarify our understanding of the way things are now being done—the operant theory—rather than articulating a proposed theory of action.

It is hard to imagine an action occurring in the schoolhouse that isn't being done for a reason. But oftentimes, things have been done a certain way for so long that it has been years since people stopped to consider and reflect on the rationale. To make an implicit theory of action explicit, action researchers conducting descriptive studies go through the same four-step process but do so in a slightly different way.

Step 1: Brainstorming the Critical Independent Variables

Generate a list of items by responding to the following question:

What issues, factors, programs, and processes are currently consuming most of our time and energy with this target?

Step 2: Summarizing the Independent Variables

State in a narrative form the actions that make up the work that is currently being done in pursuit of the target.

Step 3: Conducting an Intuitive Regression Analysis

Now we need to ask how time is currently being spent. Look over your list (Step 1) and your narrative (Step 2) for each item. Estimate the approximate percentage of the available time and energy that *is currently being devoted to* this item. The total must equal but not exceed 100%.

Step 4: Graphically Displaying the Operant Theory

Draw the information from Step 3 in the form of a pie graph and explain the relative percentages. Be careful to avoid using interpretive language. Rather than saying, "We are spending an enormous amount of time on x" or "We are overly emphasizing the use of worksheets instead of teacher-generated examples," try to say it like this: "We are spending 75% of our time on x" or "Of the assignments used, 80% involve publisher-supplied worksheets while a little less than 10% are teacher-developed assignments."

Occasionally, someone anticipates that he or she will be doing descriptive research, but then as the person makes the operant theory explicit, he or she becomes very uncomfortable with what is going on and immediately decides that a better theory must exist or could easily be created. When this occurs, it is a wise to go back and see if another priority pie can be created that will illustrate an improved and novel theory, using the four-step priority pie process.

Action researchers are encouraged to use a visual technique called the *graphic reconstruction* to assist with planning and further clarifying their emerging theories of action. In Chapter 5, we explore its creation and use.

5

Drawing a
Theory in Action

Let's expand the travel metaphor. As action researchers, we are traveling to distant lands, and in a larger sense we are planning on exploring territory where no one has gone before, at least not successfully. This is neither an exaggeration nor is it self-congratulatory.

As we know, if what you are attempting to accomplish had already been accomplished in a setting like yours, had been documented and was well understood, it would be a waste of your time and energy to replicate it. In all probability you are already using the best strategies and following the most promising practices you are aware of. In addition, you wouldn't be attempting something new or examining your current work were you not at least somewhat dissatisfied with the results you have been getting with those best practices. Perhaps, as a result of your literature review (see Chapter 3), you found yourself inspired by the ideas and experiences of others. Let's even say you have now decided to focus your action research on determining if some of those ideas will work with your students and your classes. But even if that is the case, you are still thinking about exploring territory where no one has gone before, because even if the promising approach has been documented, it has not been attempted in the exact manner you have in mind, in the precise context where you plan to implement it, or with students just like yours.

In Chapter 4, the priority pie was used to help you identify some of the specific categories of action that you should attend to. You identified these by combining what you had learned from the wisdom of your practice, with the experience of others, and created a prioritized list of independent variables. In all likelihood, the list of variables you ended up with (your slices of pie) didn't depart radically from your current menu of action. Perhaps you added a slice or changed your views on the relative importance of a particular category of action. Nevertheless, regardless of how deeply you believe in the narrative statement you wrote to explain your pie, that statement alone probably won't convince you (or your students, their parents, or your colleagues) that you have discovered the approach that will succeed where all others have failed. This brings us to the need for detailing a comprehensive theory of action—what I often call an implementation road map. Action researchers call this kind of map a *graphic reconstruction*. While geographic maps illuminate the relationships among landforms, the maps we will be drawing will show the relationships among actions.

■ WHY A MAP?

The map is the lifeline of the explorer. The route an explorer sets out to follow is informed by the best maps of others and the best descriptions of the terrain to be encountered that could be gleaned from those with personal knowledge of the territory. On returning from their journeys, explorers share what they have learned by modifying and adjusting the best previous map, augmented with their new knowledge. This is precisely what we shall do. We begin by developing an initial road map informed by a combination of our experience and the experience of others. The map we prepare becomes our guide as we travel to places where we haven't ventured before. To the degree that our maps are clear and appear accurate, containing what researchers call *face validity*, the greater the chance we can approach our adventure with confidence and purpose.

Christopher Columbus: An Early Action Researcher

Action research is not a new idea. Occasionally, I have argued that one can trace action research back at least as far as the three voyages of Christopher Columbus. In my retelling of history, Chris Columbus was actually an ambitious teacher, probably a high school marketing instructor. One morning he awoke with a terrific idea for a new course. He did a little library research and then developed what appeared to be a good hypothesis and emergent theory:

> If I sail due West of Spain for approximately 4,000 miles, I will land on the East Coast of Cathay. I believe this to be the case for two reasons. I know the Earth is round (actually, so did most European and Arab cartographers of the day), and I even know its circumference (also known through the use of celestial projection). When Marco Polo came back from Cathay with all that good stuff to sell, he told us how far he had traveled. I simply subtracted the distance he went from the circumference of the Earth and it became clear to me that 4,000 nautical miles will complete the circle.

So Chris went to his co-principals, Ferdinand and Isabella, and asked them to approve a budget for this new course proposal. Assuming that, as tight-fisted monarchs, they would want to pour over the details of his proposal, I imagine them demanding that Columbus provide a graphic reconstruction before granting permission for the new course. Recently, I did a literature review of my own to see if I could locate the type of graphic reconstruction Columbus might have used to illustrate his theory to his two authoritarian school administrators. Figure 5.1 is a map of the world produced by Henricus Martellus in 1489, a mere 3 years before Columbus's first voyage. As this was the most accurate map I could locate from a European cartographer of this time period, I assume that it is similar to one that Columbus might have used.

Figure 5.1   Henricus Martellus' 1489 Map

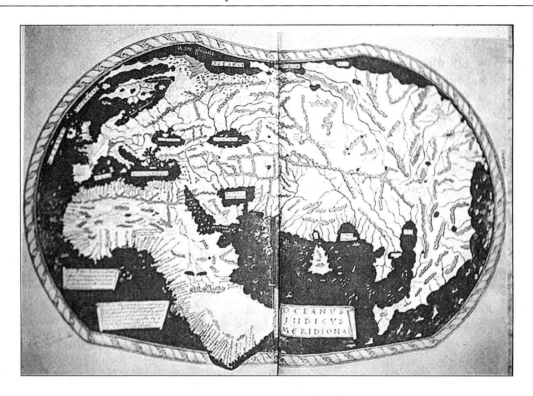

SOURCE: http://www.henry-davis.com/MAPS/LMwebpages/256.html

In my imagination, I see Columbus placing this map on an overhead projector, taking out a felt-tip marker, and inserting a line from the West Coast of Spain to the left-hand edge of the map and another one from East Asia to the other edge of the map, to illustrate his proposal. Now that we've seen how well this process worked for Christopher Columbus, it is time for you to prepare a map for your journey.

BUILDING A GRAPHIC RECONSTRUCTION ■

In Chapter 4, we looked at a priority pie prepared by middle school English teacher, Mr. Seeker, to illustrate his view of the salience of the key independent variables that he theorized should be addressed if his students were to become proficient writers of five-paragraph persuasive essays. To recap, these were the items:

Direct instruction in

- Vocabulary, word choice
- Editing skill
- Voice
- Mechanics and grammar

Feedback on

- Vocabulary, word choice
- Editing skill
- Voice
- Mechanics and grammar

Now it's time to focus on some additional questions, ones that might have been raised yet could not have been fully answered through the priority pie process. For example, Mr. Seeker might have questions regarding the *sequence* of his actions:

- Should vocabulary be taught before introducing the concept of voice?
- Should he introduce the concept of voice prior to instruction in vocabulary?
- Should these two elements of writing be taught simultaneously?

Then there could be questions regarding *instructional strategies,* such as

- Should he provide students with a vocabulary list?
- Should he ask students to identify and pull new vocabulary words from their readings?
- How and when should he provide students with feedback?

It is likely that he has many other questions about his emerging theory, such as the following:

- Who should be responsible for what?
  - Should he assume the role of editor of student drafts?
  - Should he teach the students to edit their own work and then make them responsible for editing the work?
  - Should he teach the students to work cooperatively and revise their work in peer editing groups?

While the priority pie was valuable in identifying the areas where Mr. Seeker needed to focus his energy, it didn't provide him with any meaningful guidance on how he ought to respond to these or other relevant procedural questions.

Whether your study is designed to be a quasi-experimental inquiry or a descriptive study, it is important that you go through a process to clarify in detail the specific theory of action that will be examined by your study, whether it is one you invented or one that is already in operation.

■ GRAPHIC RECONSTRUCTIONS FOR QUASI-EXPERIMENTAL RESEARCH

When undertaking quasi-experimental research, it is essential to carefully articulate precisely what we are attempting and why we are attempting to do it in a particular way. In my revisionist history, Christopher Columbus was clearly conducting quasi-experimental research. As quasi-experimental researchers, we need to spell out the proposed actions for a number of reasons:

1. *To provide guidance to others:* In Columbus's case, this would be for future seafarers and explorers.

2. *To provide insights into the experimental process:* In Columbus's case, these insights would assist him in his future explorations.

3. *To make our program clear to stakeholders:* In Columbus's case, this would be necessary to keep his benefactors happy and to keep him funded.

To Provide Guidance to Others

When we engage in experimental or quasi-experimental research, we are, of course, hoping to find evidence that supports our hypotheses regarding the specific interventions we are attempting and their relationships to changes in our achievement targets. Should we be successful and the data confirm our hypotheses, it is to be expected that others will want to try to replicate our results. If those following in our footsteps are to have confidence in their ability to confirm our findings, they will need to clearly understand the procedures we followed.

To Provide Insights Into the Process

Even the most well-thought-out interventions rarely work precisely as expected. Occasionally, this means that the theory of action was fatally flawed. More likely, it was because one or two relatively minor aspects of the plan didn't work as anticipated. Unless each and every aspect of the plan had been clearly delineated, it would be impossible to determine where exactly the breakdown occurred. This is no small problem. In schools, this is often played out when an adopted program has been evaluated, deemed ineffective, and then tossed out. When this occurs without serious reflection on the reason for the lack of success, it can seriously erode staff commitment to the entire process of innovation.

In all likelihood, the packaged program arrived without an explicit theory of action delineated by the developer or publisher. The district's justification for implementing the program was probably stated in shorthand and simply mentioned the name of the publisher:

> After reviewing the available materials, we decided to teach reading with the Sagor reading series.

Such a theory could be depicted like this:

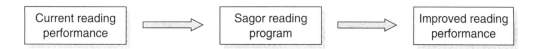

If performance didn't live up to the district's expectations, one would expect to hear the assertion, "The Sagor program didn't work." Consequently, the program would be abandoned, another one would be adopted, and the cycle would continue. Occasionally, throwing away programs that failed to live up to expectations is warranted; but often, it is not. Frequently, the program that was adopted was fundamentally sound. In all likelihood, a few specific aspects of the program weren't adequate to meet the needs of the district's students. Certainly it would be more efficient as well as more intellectually honest to isolate the particular flawed aspects of the program so they could be modified, adjusted, or supplemented, rather than throwing out the baby with the bathwater and starting all over again.

However, if the interventions implemented are simply viewed as mysterious black boxes, it becomes impossible to determine what needs to be modified. When the process of adopt-evaluate-replace-adopt-evaluate-replace repeats itself over and over, it produces a syndrome of revolving-door programs that can breed cynicism and defeatism. We can all agree that those two attitudes serve no one well in the modern schoolhouse.

The same thing applies to your action research. More likely than not, your well-conceived theories of action will be fundamentally sound. If you don't obtain the results you expect, yet you follow a detailed plan of action, you will be able to conduct a detailed academic postmortem on your actions and determine where things went awry.

To Make the Program Clear to Stakeholders

When students and families clearly understand the programs they are involved with and can see the rationale for the tasks they are being asked to complete, they are more likely to cooperate and give their best efforts. Conversely, when students feel they are being asked to do something new and out of the ordinary and the only rationale they are offered for doing it in a particular way is because, "I said so," they can be expected to rebel or give the program something less than their best efforts. For this reason, I have made it a habit to share my theories of action by distributing copies of graphic reconstructions on the first day of class for any new programs that I will be implementing.

■ GRAPHIC RECONSTRUCTIONS WITH DESCRIPTIVE RESEARCH

When engaging in descriptive research, our primary purpose is to develop a deeper understanding of what is actually going on here and now. If our search is to succeed in answering that question, we need to have some good ideas about where to look to collect our data. An efficient strategy is to invest a little time at the outset, reflecting on the rationale for the actions (the operant theory) that are currently occurring, and use the results of that reflection to help focus our data collection. Frequently, a review of the teacher's manual or curriculum guides provides some insight on what actions are *supposed* to be occurring.

Why Is It Important to Plan Visually?

When discussing something familiar, we often take intellectual shortcuts without even noticing them. For example, when outstanding teachers are asked to explain precisely what they do to produce the results they are obtaining, they often are at a loss to explain their successes. We might hear an explanation like, "This is just how my students perform." Of course, this is an inadequate explanation. No doubt, there are certain specific actions the teacher consistently does that lead to these results, but by now they have become second nature and so aren't even recognized as relevant.

Graphic reconstructions help us flesh out the details of our theories of action by using a less familiar language: visualizations or pictures. The graphic reconstruction is a flow chart, a web that illustrates the dynamic relationships that exist between the various components of a theory of action. Figure 5.2 shows the graphic reconstruction produced by Mr. Seeker, illustrating his theory for improving his students' persuasive essays. Figure 5.3 reflects Dr. Hernandez's theory on enhancing the problem-solving capacity of her school's faculty.

Figure 5.2 Enhancing Student Persuasive Writing

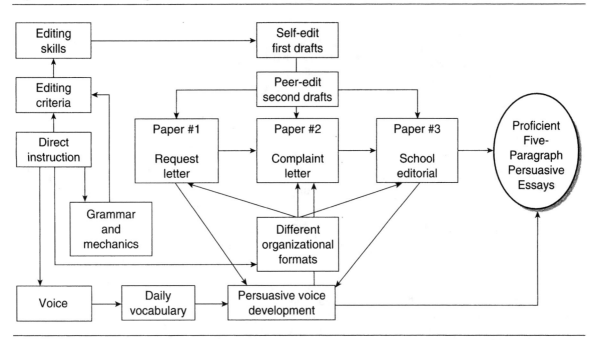

There is no single way to build a graphic reconstruction, and there is no single layout that will be effective in illustrating all theories. If this is your first time creating a graphic reconstruction, you should find the following five steps helpful for developing the visual road map of the theory of action you plan to investigate.

1. Brainstorming ideas

2. Grouping and sorting ideas and activities

3. Putting them in sequence

4. Proofing the roadmap

5. Reviewing the final product

To demonstrate the use of these five steps, let's follow a hypothetical middle school faculty that is creating a graphic reconstruction to clarify their theory on a schoolwide program target: improving student motivation. Figure 5.4 shows the priority pie and narrative created earlier by this faculty.

Keeping the emergent theory as illustrated by the pie and narrative in mind, this faculty is now ready to start building their graphic reconstruction.

Step 1: Brainstorming

Using a pad of Post-it notes, the action researchers brainstorm every factor, issue, phenomenon, program, and practice that they believe has a bearing on the target being pursued. This includes ideas that surfaced during the literature review as well as items that showed up as separate slices of their priority pie. It is important to be expansive when brainstorming. Action researchers are wise to include things they've discovered through personal experience as well as things gleaned from the literature.

Figure 5.3 Enhancing Problem-Solving Capacity

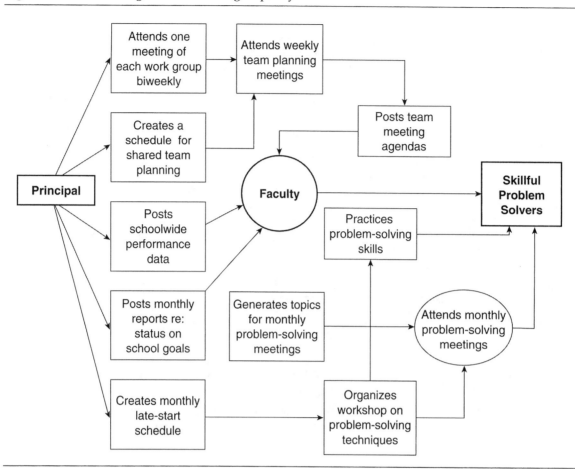

Figure 5.4 Building Motivated Learners

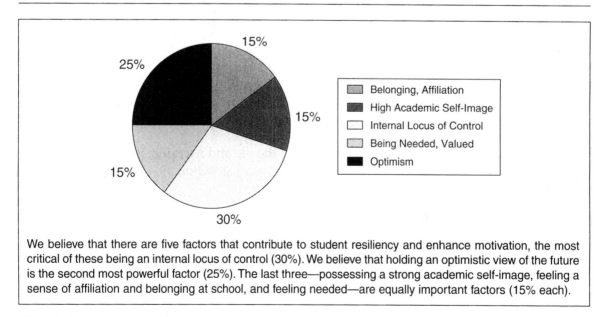

These are some of the items that might have surfaced in the brainstorming regarding enhancing motivation:

- Cooperative learning
- Learning-style-friendly classes
- Feelings of competence
- External locus of control
- Teacher advisory program
- Problem-solving discipline practices
- Feelings of belonging
- Curricula emphasizing cause and effect
- Feelings of usefulness
- Internal locus of control
- Feelings of potency
- Service learning
- Project-based learning
- Feelings of alienation
- Feeling unneeded
- Mastery expectations

Step 2: Grouping and Sorting the Items

Once brainstorming is completed, it is time to spread the Post-it notes out on a table or a piece of chart paper and cluster them into related groups. Some of the grouping strategies that I've found helpful are

- Problems, interventions, and targets
- Prior to teaching, during teaching, after teaching
- Teacher actions, student actions

Keep in mind there is no one way to categorize the ideas that surface during brainstorming. Play around with different categories until you find one that best helps you organize your ideas.

The team working on enhancing motivation decided to sort their items as *problems, interventions, and targets:*

Problems

- Low academic self-image
- Feelings of alienation
- Feeling unneeded
- External locus of control (feeling powerless)

Interventions

- Service learning
- Cooperative learning
- Mastery expectations
- Project-based learning

- Teacher advisory
- Learning-style-friendly classes
- Problem-solving discipline
- Curricula emphasizing cause and effect

Targets

- Feeling useful
- Feeling optimistic
- Feeling of belonging
- Feeling potent (internal locus of control)
- Feeling competent

Step 3: Putting the Items in Sequence

In this step, the Post-it notes are arranged to illustrate inferred relationships. This is generally done using a large sheet of poster paper or chart-pak. For quasi-experimental research I organize my graphic this way: On the left-hand side, I group the items that describe the current situation or problem my actions are designed to address. For the student motivation project, the left side of the graphic would look like Figure 5.5.

Then on the right-hand side, I put my vision of success, the Promised Land I am in pursuit of. Here I place descriptions of performance on the target that is at or above expected proficiency (at or above the midpoint on the rating scales developed in Chapter 2). When those Post-its are added to the motivation graphic, it would look like Figure 5.6.

The last step is to arrange all the other items (i.e., the solutions or actions) in a manner that reflects the most logical and direct route that I see the program or the learners taking to get from the current situation to the target. Once the interventions have been added, the complete graphic for the enhancing motivation project would look like Figure 5.7.

In a quasi-experimental study, the researcher often assumes that there is a sequence for the activities and may infer causal relationships. It can be helpful to use lines or directional arrows to illustrate how different elements of the theory build on or impact each other. However, linear indicators are not always useful. Particularly when working with early learners, instructional activities frequently are cyclical and repeated.

Arranging the items for a descriptive study often tends to be more idiosyncratic. It is important that the graphic for a descriptive study illustrates all the phenomena that the researcher believes are relevant to the topic and are likely to be present or could be observed in the environment being studied. It is critically important to identify these items at this point, as later on they will form the basis for data collection.

> The locations where items are placed on the descriptive graphic can be important if they help inform the researcher where and perhaps when to look for data. Beyond that, determining the possible or probable relationships between items or variables is not that crucial for a descriptive study.

This part of the process is complete when the researchers are able to step back and look at their graphic reconstruction and declare that it clearly and unambiguously

Figure 5.5   Building Motivated Learners

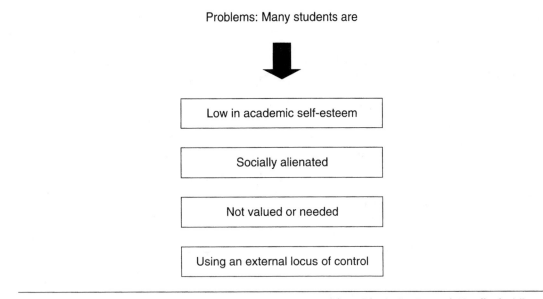

Problems: Many students are

Low in academic self-esteem

Socially alienated

Not valued or needed

Using an external locus of control

Copyright © 2005 Corwin Press. All rights reserved. Reprinted from *The Action Research Handbook: A Four-Step Process for Educators and School Teams,* by Richard Sagor. Thousand Oaks, CA: Corwin Press, www .corwinpress.com. Reproduction authorized only for the local school site that has purchased this book.

Figure 5.6   Building Motivated Learners: Targets

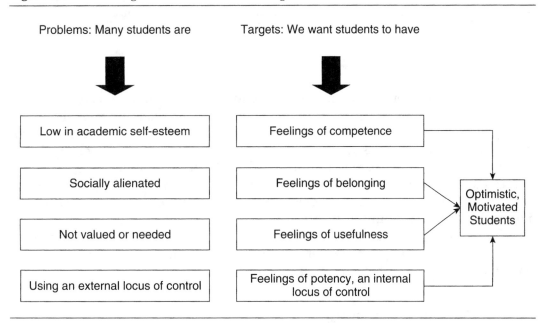

Problems: Many students are   Targets: We want students to have

Low in academic self-esteem   Feelings of competence

Socially alienated   Feelings of belonging

Not valued or needed   Feelings of usefulness   Optimistic, Motivated Students

Using an external locus of control   Feelings of potency, an internal locus of control

illustrates their understanding of the dynamics of the issue being studied, the independent variables (the actions), and the dependent variable (the achievement target).

When I think I am at this point, I imagine myself explaining my graphic to three particular audiences: my students, their parents, and a new person on the faculty. If

Figure 5.7   Building Motivated Learners: Complete

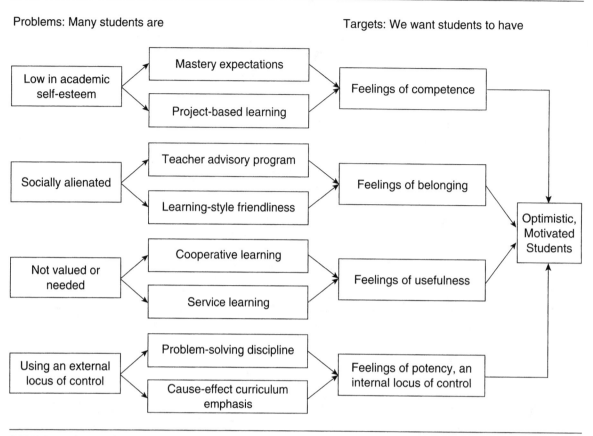

SOURCE: Adapted from Sagor (1996), Figure 4.4.

my graphic is complete and clear when accompanied by a 5-minute verbal explanation, my students should be able to understand what I am planning and will be able to paraphrase my theory in their own words. Likewise, if after a 5-minute explanation at an open house, parents understand what I have planned and feel capable of explaining it to another parent, I can be confident that my graphic has successfully communicated my theory. Last, if an educator new to our team could understand the program we are planning to implement after a short review, I would feel we had illustrated our ideas with clarity. But if the graphic plus a short explanation didn't clarify what was planned and its rationale, then I would have to assume that it is still too abstract or overly general. When that occurs, I continue to work on refining the road map until it has achieved the clarity I'm after.

Step 4: Proofing the Graphic

Once Step 3 is completed and I am confident that the graphic reconstruction successfully communicates my ideas, it is time for me to search for flaws. The way I do this is to think of as diverse a range of kids as I might ever have in class. Then I mentally walk through my graphic several times as though it was a trail. Each time I walk the trail, I think of a particular category of student and imagine them experiencing the program as it is illustrated. As I take these walks, I try to identify any places where students such as these might encounter problems or get lost, based on my past experience. This is analogous to drawing a map for a person who will be making a first visit to your home. Prior to sending out your map, you will probably go over it one last time, looking for places where you might expect someone who is unfamiliar with your neighborhood to make a wrong turn.

When the teachers who were working on the motivation project did this proofing, they were able to quickly spot several problems. For example, their graphic (Figure 5.7) implied that the requirement of having students meet mastery expectations (academic credit only awarded for grades of A or B) would lead to increased feelings of competence. But when they walked through their theory in the shoes of a student with a history of easily giving up, they realized that students such as this would likely find mastery expectations so intimidating that they might just stop trying—and consequently never hit the target of increased feelings of competence.

Another example involves the inferred relationship between a teacher advisory program and the development of feelings of belonging. Their theory of action implied that having a teacher advisor would increase a student's feelings of belonging at school. But in the proofing exercise, the teachers could identify many categories of students who they felt wouldn't thrive in an advisory program. They worried that if the interpersonal chemistry wasn't right between students and their advisors or between students and their peers in the advisory group, the advisory process might serve to make them even more alienated than they were before.

When problems like these turn up when proofing the graphic, it is time to reflect on the following question:

How could the theory of action be modified to make universal success more likely?

After spending some time reflecting on that question, it is time to work those changes into the theory. With the motivation project, the teachers decided to create an after-school academic coaching program staffed with charismatic teachers and involving lots of fun activities as a venue for students who needed extra help to achieve mastery. They also added a process whereby school counselors would play a role in matching students to advisors and arbitrating problems when and if they arose. Figure 5.8 shows the revised graphic after these modifications were added.

Step 5: Finalizing the Graphic

For quasi–experimental research, the graphic reconstruction can be declared complete once the researchers can say, "We truly expect that every student will experience success if this theory of action is implemented as displayed."

For descriptive research, the graphic can be considered complete when the researchers can say, "We believe that once we come to understand how all the elements displayed on this graphic work and interact with each other, we will understand why performance is as it currently is."

When doing descriptive research on a commercially produced program or the implementation of an adopted program, it is a good idea to follow the steps provided in this chapter to construct a graphic reconstruction of the theory of action *as you currently understand it.* Then prior to commencing your study, ask the developers of the program or their representatives to take a critical look at your graphic and provide feedback. Even if you are aware that some elements of the theory as originally conceived by the authors or developers aren't present in your classroom or program, understanding those differences in theoretical perspective may prove helpful when you are doing data analysis.

Figure 5.8 Building Motivated Learners: After Proofing

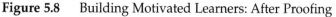

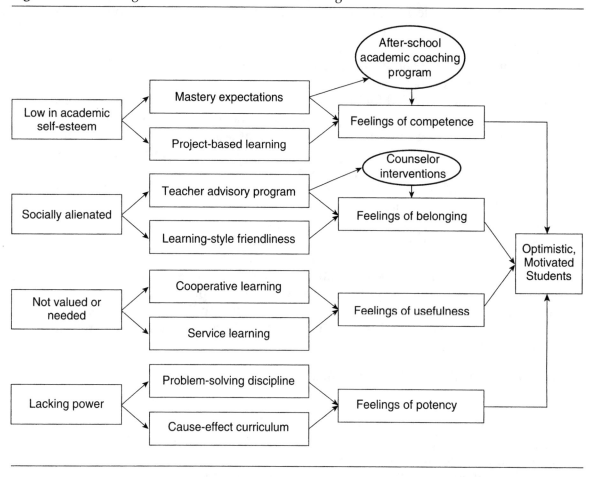

When you have finished producing a graphic reconstruction that reflects your understanding of the issue under study, it is time to pat yourself on the back. You have completed Stage 2: Articulating Your Theory, and you are almost ready to move to the exciting implementation-action phase of the action research process.

6

Determining the
Research Questions

Now that you have completed a graphic reconstruction that clearly communicates your best and most current thinking on how to achieve success with your priority achievement targets, you have completed the second of the four stages of the action research process.

You have finally arrived at the *action* portion, where you will be *implementing* or *exploring* your theory of action. Two things occur simultaneously while you engage in Stage 3 work:

1. Your theory of action is implemented.

2. Data is collected in response to a set of meaningful research questions.

The nature of the research questions influences both the types of data to be collected and the methods used to collect them. So it is extremely important that care and thought be used in choosing the questions that will guide the inquiry. Just as it is important to choose a focus near the top of your personal priority list (Chapter 2), selecting the questions that will guide your inquiry should be grounded in professional self-interest: A good action research question is one that leads to greater understanding of something you very much *need* or *want* to learn more about.

In this chapter, we will examine two approaches to the selection of research questions. The first involves a set of generic action research questions and applying it to the issue you are studying. The data produced in response to these questions provides the information needed by most action researchers conducting quasi-experimental as well as descriptive inquiries. The second approach is a process that helps you systematically analyze your theory of action to tease out specific questions with potential for uncovering personally and professionally meaningful information.

■ THREE GENERIC ACTION RESEARCH QUESTIONS

The range and scope of questions an action researcher might wish to pursue is unlimited. Nevertheless, there are three particular questions that can provide valuable professional insight when used with nearly any project. They are the following:

- What did I or we actually do? (This focuses on action.)
- What *changes* occurred regarding performance on the achievement targets? (This focuses on change.)
- What were the *relationships,* if any, between the actions taken and the changes in performance? (This focuses on relationships.)

I refer to these generic action research questions by the acronym ACR, which refers to their foci: "A" for action, "C" for change, and "R" for relationships. Let's examine the ACR questions to determine if they can help you get the answers and insights *you want and need.*

ACR Question 1: What Did I or We Actually Do?

On the surface, this question seems so mundane that it is often overlooked, and the novice action researcher occasionally fails to collect the data needed to provide an adequate answer. Not knowing the answer to this question can create a significant problem during the final stage of the process (reflection and action planning). The essential rationale for asking and answering this question can be found in Newton's first law of motion:

For every action there is an equal or opposite reaction.

Whatever happens in our schools or classrooms was influenced by an earlier action or, more realistically, by a collection of actions. Knowing what precipitated an occurrence allows us to predict, with varying degrees of confidence, what might happen in the future. However, if we are unclear about the precipitating events, our ability to predict an event or replicate results can be very difficult. This is not just an abstract or theoretical issue. It is a matter of real consequence.

In Chapter 5, we discussed the recurring problem of discontinuing fundamentally sound programs because of an initial failure to produce the desired results. This resulted from a set of understandable circumstances. Individual teachers, schools, and districts adopt programs because they believe these programs hold promise for improving student performance. Then, after a year or two of implementation, the programs are deemed failures and are discontinued. The justification for ending the programs is simple and straightforward: After implementation, the anticipated outcomes weren't realized. Such a decision would be perfectly reasonable, assuming the program had been, in fact, actually implemented and implemented appropriately. Unfortunately, just because a program was adopted or was tried doesn't necessarily mean it was implemented as intended, in accordance with the developer's theory of action.

This lesson was driven home for me a few years ago when a team of elementary school teachers came to an action research training program I was conducting. Their superintendent had asked them to investigate the effectiveness of a very expensive and complex literacy program adopted in their district 3 years earlier. The program had been brought in with much fanfare and with high expectations for spurring improvement in the district's reading performance. The program included texts, videos, workbooks, and a host of other supplemental materials. While expensive, the program appeared to be well worth the money when one considered its promise for improving reading scores. After 3 years of use, however, there had been no significant change in student performance on the state reading exam. It was no surprise that this team came to the action research training with a research question already in hand. They wanted to know if the adopted program was worth it. As much as it had cost to purchase the program materials, the superintendent was willing to admit the mistake, move on, and try another strategy if it was determined that the adoption was, indeed, a mistake.

When developing a data-collection plan to help answer their question, these teacher researchers decided to create and analyze *curriculum maps.* The process they used had every elementary teacher record which portions of the program they had been using as well as the amount of time they were devoting to the various program components. When this implementation data was charted, the team noticed something right away.

Apparently, each teacher had selected which program components to use and even more important, which components to ignore, idiosyncratically, based on personal bias or taste. Many teachers omitted entire portions of the program, while others gave some components minimal attention and spent considerable time with other parts. There was no common pattern of use, even across the same grade level in the same school. As a consequence, in a typical class, a teacher might find some students who had considerable previous experience with certain portions of the program sitting next to classmates who had never encountered that particular aspect of the same program. Once this data was analyzed, it became clear that no teacher in the district could fairly assume that any two students had been through the same scope and sequence.

When the superintendent asked the research team to report what they learned from their study, he expected one of two answers to his original question:

1. The program was shown to be a worthy one and had, in reality, succeeded in improving student performance in reading.

2. The program had not delivered on its promise for improving performance.

But the research team determined that the data couldn't support either of those conclusions and clearly reported something quite different: *Few, if any, students had actually experienced the program as it was intended.* Therefore, they told the superintendent they couldn't evaluate the program's effectiveness (the adequacy of the program's theory of action) since it hadn't been properly implemented.

Neglecting to collect data to determine what was actually implemented can be costly in dollars, time, and missed opportunity.

In Chapters 4 and 5, we made our theories of action explicit by producing detailed graphic reconstructions and estimating the amounts of time and energy needed to achieve success (the priority pie). When we get to Stage 4, we will want to be able to draw conclusions about the adequacy of these theories. To do so, we need to establish and document the specific actions that we took and what was experienced by our students. Fortunately, gathering this data is relatively easy.

Teachers develop and keep track of what they intend to teach and what they expect the students to experience. Our weekly lesson plan books contain all this data. However, the lesson plan book alone often may not have accurate enough information to adequately answer ACR Question 1. Using myself as an example, it was the very rare week when the activities I anticipated doing and wrote as lesson plans on Sunday night actually matched what I taught and what my students experienced during the ensuing week. I make no apologies for this. Like most teachers, I willingly and readily adjusted my plans based on circumstances and student needs. I added additional time for work on skills that weren't being acquired, and I struck activities that seem redundant and appeared to be a waste of time. So although my plans were written with sincerity and represented what I thought I would do, they couldn't produce an accurate record of what had actually occurred. This problem can be easily remedied. All that is required is allocating 5 minutes each Friday afternoon to go over the past week's plans and adjust them to reflect what actually transpired. Figure 6.1 is an illustration of a week's lesson plans annotated by the teacher to reflect what really happened.

By engaging in this one simple additional piece of record keeping, I can end the school year with a complete record of what actions occurred on each of the 180 days in my classroom. Furthermore, by correlating this data with attendance records, I can create an accurate report on which specific activities were experienced by each individual student. Later, should I find myself pleased with the learning that occurred, I can track the precise instructional activities that corresponded with that learning. Conversely, if I am disappointed with student performance, I will be in possession of an accurate record of what events coincided with the less than stellar results.

An additional record-keeping devise that I have found helpful is the Time Priority Tracking Form (Figure 6.2). On this form, you write each category of action that appeared on your priority pie (see Chapter 4). Then, after reviewing your weekly activities, write the approximate amount of time spent during that week on each of the categories of action. Later, when you are analyzing your data, you will be able to see how closely the percentages of time spent compare to what you had anticipated would be required.

ACR Question 2: What Changes Occurred Regarding Performance on the Achievement Targets?

If you were pleased with the rating scales and rate-of-growth charts you developed in Chapter 3, you probably want to use them to monitor changes in performance as they occur, with your priority achievement targets. As happy as you may be with the measuring tools you produced, you still ought to be suspicious of drawing conclusions regarding student performance from any single source of data. Putting that much weight on one set of data is equivalent to a prosecutor, responsible for proving a case beyond a reasonable doubt, betting everything on the testimony of a single witness. Most trial lawyers would not rest a case on only one witness's testimony, regardless of how honorable and credible that witness may be. This is because they know that a jury, which might believe in the integrity of the witness, could still have justifiable concerns about the possibility that the witness was confused or otherwise mistaken. This is why lawyers always seek corroborating testimony. That is also a good approach for an action researcher. When we assemble data to answer ACR Question 2, it behooves us to look for several *separate* and *independent* sources for information on changes in the performance on each priority achievement target.

Fortunately, locating multiple sources of data on performance isn't overly problematic. For example, if I want to know if my students have learned the proper use of writing conventions, I might assess this by having them edit a sample piece of

Figure 6.1 Lesson Plan for Week of October 15

Subject: Government

Section: Sixth Period

Monday	Tuesday	Wednesday	Thursday	Friday
Write in current events journals (10 minutes). Discuss initiative petition process. Review arguments pro and con in voters' pamphlets. Discuss initiatives #118, #217, and #482. Homework: Read essay, "Direct vs Representative Democracy."	Pop quiz on homework. Class debate: Be it resolved that representative student government should be abolished. Random assignment to teams, draw debaters from hat. 20 minutes preparation. 20-minute debate. Homework: Reflection worksheet	Film: *The Founding Fathers: Why a Republic?*	Direct democracy scavenger hunt. In cooperative learning teams, allow 20 minutes to find direct democracy events in past 2 months from classroom media and Internet. Compile team lists and submit by end of period.	Write in current events journals (10 minutes). Team presentations, 10 minutes per team. Work on PBL proposals.
Changes: Didn't discuss initiative #482	Changes: Didn't do debate Didn't assign homework	Changes: Didn't show film Held 20-minute debate (originally planned for Tuesday) Homework: Reflection sheet	Changes: None	Changes: None

Figure 6.2 Time Priority Tracking Sheet

Date: _____

Class: _____

Focus Area (from priority pie)	Approximate Class Time Spent (in minutes)	Comment

Copyright © 2005 Corwin Press. All rights reserved. Reprinted from *The Action Research Handbook: A Four-Step Process for Educators and School Teams*, by Richard Sagor. Thousand Oaks, CA: Corwin Press, www.corwinpress.com. Reproduction authorized only for the local school site that has purchased this book.

work where they will be required to identify and correct common convention errors. However, if later I want to make assertions about their competence, I will want to corroborate those results with other sources of data. In all likelihood, the data needed to do this already exist and are present in my classroom; therefore, no additional testing or data collection should be required. For instance, I could validate these findings with items found in their writing portfolios, where I could see whether they have been using conventions correctly in their writing. This process of using corroborating evidence to establish validity and reliability is what researchers call *triangulation*. In Chapter 7, you will be guided in developing a full-blown, triangulated data-collection plan to answer your research questions.

ACR Question 3: What Were the Relationships, if Any, Between the Actions Taken and the Changes in Performance?

Just because I can unequivocally establish what I did and what the students experienced (Question 1) and can demonstrate with confidence what the students achieved (Question 2), it doesn't mean I can claim a relationship exists between my actions and those documented changes in student performance.

Earlier we discussed the relationship between dependent and independent variables, the dependent variable being those things we wanted to see changed and the independent variables being the things we were doing in an attempt to affect that change. In the natural sciences, we observe the interaction of independent and dependent variables as a straightforward cause-and-effect relationship. Any changes observed in the dependent variable (the achievement target) can be attributed to adjustments in the independent variables. In controlled experimental conditions in the natural sciences, these are supportable conclusions, because in laboratory situations, it is possible to fully control the environment.

However, when we are dealing with human behavior and with social interactions, things can never be quite that simple and straightforward. For us to claim that "A" caused "B," we would have to be able to prove that *nothing* else could possibly have influenced the final result. Let's say my target is to have one of my students, Sam, become more diligent in editing his written work. I decide to accomplish this by prodding my students with detailed teacher feedback following the first draft of each of their essays. The data I collected have shown a clear pattern: The overall quality of the editing in Sam's final papers is much improved compared to his earlier work. The relationship seems clear to me, as shown in the following figure.

I can see that when I changed my feedback process, Sam's editing improved. From this data, I could feel confident asserting that my actions were the cause of Sam's improvement.

But I didn't realize that at the same time that I began providing intensive feedback, other factors independent of my actions also changed. Coincidental with my provision of intensive feedback, Sam's father began offering him a $25 reward for every "A" he received on a major school project. Now that I am in possession of this data, a new question has emerged: How might I determine if the improvement in Sam's work was due to my teaching or the result of his father's bribe?

Two categories of factors often interfere with a direct relationship between dependent and independent variables. Researchers call these *extraneous* and *intervening* variables. An extraneous variable is something that has nothing to do with the phenomenon being studied (my teaching) but gets in the way in a manner that influences the result. The bribe provided by Sam's dad was separate and apart from the phenomenon I was studying (the relationship between my feedback and the quality of Sam's editing), but it influenced the dependent variable being measured (the quality of Sam's final papers).

An intervening variable is a phenomenon that is also influenced by an independent variable (my intervention) while having its own separate effect on the outcome (dependent variable). For example, let's say I'm a PE teacher who notices that students whose homes are located north of the river are better golfers than students living on the south side. I conclude that housing location improves one's golf game. The causal relationship might be illustrated this way:

However, what I don't take into account is that the north end of town is where the more affluent families live, as well as where all the town's better golf courses are located. Consequently, the factor that may more powerfully influence students' skills with golf isn't their housing location; it may be the increased practice that results from access to golf courses and the financial ability to play the game, illustrated as follows:

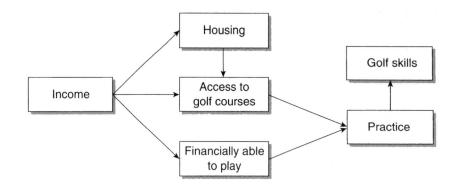

In Chapter 7, when we work on developing valid and reliable data-collection plans, we will spend considerable time on strategies designed to enhance confidence in the relationship between specific actions and documented outcomes. Having that confidence is important if we plan on revising our actions based on our data.

■ DEVELOPING YOUR OWN RESEARCH QUESTIONS

In Chapter 5, you worked through a process of articulating your theory of action. You visually illustrated your theory with an implementation road map, a graphic reconstruction. Often our theories of action are robust. By this we mean they involve dozens, sometimes even hundreds, of different assumptions. In human endeavors, nothing is ever certain. So, realistically, every item on your road map is an assumption: the role of each individual activity is an assumption, the way you sequenced the activities is based on assumptions, and the relationship of individual activities to each other and ultimately to the achievement of the priority achievement target is an assumption. As cynics like to point out, nothing in modern society is ever certain but death and taxes.

Some of the assumptions in your theory of action are right on the surface and easy to see. For example, a graphic reconstruction could contain a relationship such as is shown in the following figure.

The connection between these things is clear and direct; the action researcher is asserting a belief that there is a dynamic relationship between self-esteem and grades. But that is only the surface assumption. That same dynamic presumes numerous other underlying assumptions. For example, several of the implied assumptions in this relationship are that

- Self-esteem is important
- Grades are valuable
- Different grades are awarded to different students
- Self-esteem is malleable

As an inquiring educator, you may have an interest in investigating and developing a deeper understanding of some of those assumed relationships. But rarely is one person equally interested in or capable of exploring every one of the assumptions contained within his or her comprehensive theory of action. When one considers that there are literally hundreds of assumptions that could be investigated, the question for the part-time action researcher becomes this crucial one:

What are the specific questions that are worth spending my finite time and energy investigating?

We next explore a systematic process designed to help you go about responding to that question.

TWO-STEP WALK-THROUGH ■

The last thing you did when completing your graphic reconstruction (implementation road map) was to proof your theory by walking through the road map in the shoes of different types of students to see if you could identify obstacles or omissions and correct them. We are going to repeat that process once again, but this time you will be asking slightly different questions as you walk through your graphic reconstruction.

Hopefully, when you proofed your theory by walking through it and searching for problems, the process resulted in a final theory of action that represented your best thinking regarding a comprehensive strategy to get everyone to the desired destination. Now that you are ready to implement your theory and begin the action part of the process, there is another overriding issue you need to be concerned with: determining if your best thinking as represented in your theory of action was, in fact, adequate to succeed with your priority achievement target.

The role of your research questions is to help you accomplish that task. Earlier we said that everything on your graphic reconstruction was an assumption, and you could, if you had both the time and interest, go about systematically validating or refuting each one of these assumptions. Assuming that you do have a life outside of being an action researcher, you probably want to narrow the scope of your inquiry. The way to do this is by focusing only on the issues where you truly *need* or *want* to know more.

We will do this by walking through your theory two more times. On each walk, you will be asking yourself one of these questions:

1. Is this factor, issue, variable, or relationship significant?

2. How certain am I about the workings of this factor, issue, variable, or relationship?

Based on your answers to these two questions, one or more meaningful action research questions should emerge.

Walk-Through 1: Determining Significance

Everything that makes up your theory of action is something you believe, and everything illustrated on your graphic reconstruction is something that, in your opinion, plays a role in realizing success on the achievement target. However, as we saw when developing the priority pies, everything involved in achieving success on our targets is not of equal importance.

On this first walk-through, question the relative importance of every single element of your theory. This includes every box, circle, square, arrow, line, and so forth that appears on your graphic reconstruction. Specifically, you should ask,

Is this factor, issue, variable, and relationship significant?

To be deemed significant for our action research purposes, a factor or relationship needs to meet two qualifications. First, does this factor or relationship exercise a powerful influence over the phenomenon? For example, if our focus is on developing student self-esteem and we have an arrow that shows a relationship between "parenting skills" and "the level of self-esteem," we might conclude that this relationship qualifies as significant, meaning we believe the relationship between parenting and a child's self-esteem is a powerful one. But that is only one aspect of significance.

The second aspect refers to whether you feel this factor could be significantly influenced by *your* actions. While we deemed parenting to be a powerful factor in the development of self-esteem, we might conclude that our ability to influence the parenting received by our students is quite limited. For our purposes here, we only declare something to be significant if it qualifies under both aspects of this definition. Therefore, the relationship of parenting to self-esteem would not be classified as "significant" for purposes of teacher action research.

Now let's imagine an arrow that reflects a relationship between grades received and self-esteem. In all likelihood, we will conclude that this relationship meets both definitions of significance: it plays a powerful role in the development of self-esteem and, since grading is a practice we have control over, it is a factor that can be significantly influenced by our actions.

Figure 6.3 is a graphic reconstruction created by a hypothetical fifth-grade teacher, whom we shall call Ms. Pioneer. It illustrates her plan to use cooperative teaming to help her students hit two priority achievement targets: learning to contribute to meaningful cooperative work, and producing quality multimedia projects. Those components of her theory that she deemed significant are indicated with the letter "S." It isn't surprising that she identified 15 of the *elements* and 5 of the *relationships* illustrated on her theory as significant. (We generally find significance in

Figure 6.3 Second-Quarter Group Projects: Social Studies—Walk-Through 1

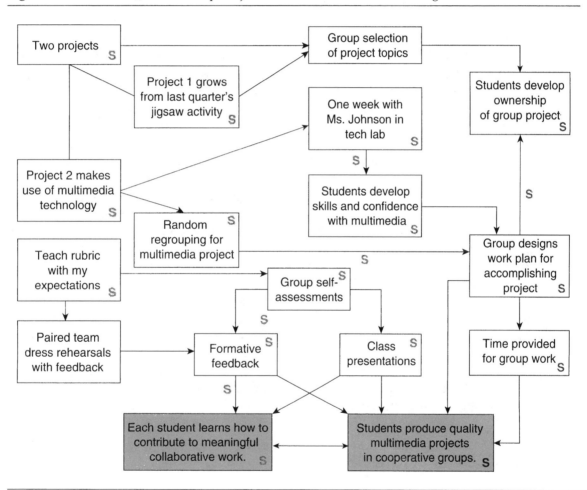

most components of a theory we authored, since instinctively, we focused on issues we deemed important when designing our theory.)

Your task now is to take out a copy of your graphic reconstruction and ask Question 1 of every single item (box, cluster of boxes, arrows, etc.) that makes up your theory. Then indicate your judgment on significance by writing an "S" by or on every item that meets the two-part definition.

Aspects of your theory that you designate as significant could very well be worth spending time investigating. Other aspects of the theory, those that didn't meet the definition of significance, shouldn't be dropped from the theory, and they should stay where they are on your graphic reconstruction, but in all likelihood, they don't justify further investments of the limited time and energy you have available for data collection.

Walk-Through 2: Your Confidence in the Assumptions

Now walk through your theory a second time; however, this time, only consider those aspects of your theory that were deemed to be significant. The question you will be asking of these items is,

How sure am I about the workings of this factor, variable, or relationship?

No doubt there will be some factors or relationships about which you are quite confident, such as the earlier example of the relationship between self-esteem and grades. While you might have already decided that this is a significant relationship, are you quite confident that you understand the workings of this phenomenon? It is possible that you have a great deal of confidence in this assumption, and there are a number of things that could justify this confidence. For example, when you did your literature review, you may have read considerable research on the role of grades and self-esteem, or the source of your confidence could be from your years of personal experience.

Alternatively, as you reflect on this question, you might conclude that while you feel this is a matter of significance and you *believe* this assumption is correct, you recognize that it is still only conjecture and you could well be mistaken. When this is the case, indicate your uncertainty by placing the letter "U" next to the "S."

Once you've completed the second walk-through, your graphic reconstruction probably has several items marked with an "SU," factors that you have deemed both *significant* and about which you are *relatively uncertain.* Figure 6.4 is Ms. Pioneer's graphic reconstruction after her second walk-through.

Significant issues that you are uncertain about are precisely the things that justify an investment of your finite professional time and energy. The only task left is to take the items that were flagged during the two-step walk-through and word them as action research questions. Figure 6.5 shows a list of 13 elements and 5 relationships that Ms. Pioneer identified as significant. The elements and relationships in bold print are those that were deemed both significant and uncertain and consequently worthy of incorporating into research questions.

■ DRAFTING THE QUESTIONS

The way a research question is worded is not just a matter of semantics. Wording can make a big difference, because precise wording of the question plays a role in determining the type of data that will be needed to provide an adequate answer. A set of guidelines follows, for your consideration while drafting your action research questions.

- *Avoid narrow questions that could be answered yes or no* (e.g., Does teacher feedback influence student motivation?). One way to determine if a question is too narrow is to ask yourself,

Will a definitive answer to this question, in itself, provide helpful direction for further action?

Figure 6.4   Second-Quarter Group Projects: Social Studies—Walk-Through 2

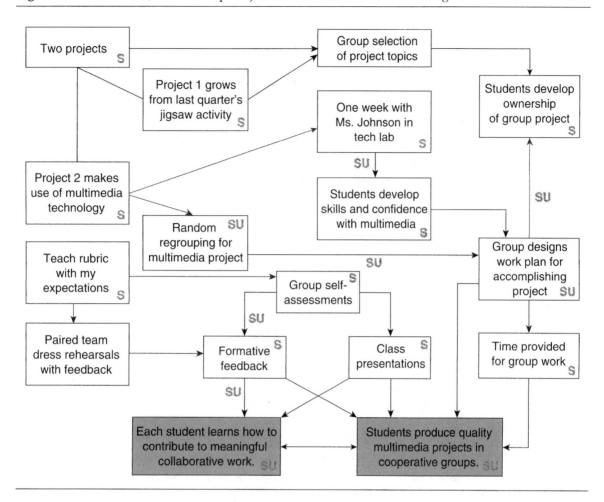

Let's assume the answer to the example given was

Yes, teacher feedback influences student motivation.

Would you say that this answer provides the direction you need to plan your next steps and which actions to take? Probably not. This is because the simple "yes" answer neither illustrated how and why feedback influences motivation nor how different forms of feedback might influence motivation.

• *Do ask open-ended questions, where a large number of potential answers may surface* (e.g., What are the relationships of different forms of feedback to changes in student performance?).

When this question is evaluated through the criteria of its *potential for informing future action,* one would be much happier with the result. This is because the data collected in answer to that question will undoubtedly provide insights into the specific nature of feedback a teacher ought to consider using when trying to enhance student motivation in the future.

• *Avoid using causal language.* Many beginning action researchers feel that conducting scientific research means uncovering definitive cause-and-effect relationships. This is understandable. Most of us learned about what constitutes

Figure 6.5   Significant Aspects of Theory and Significant Relationships

---

Significant Aspects of Theory

1. That there be two projects
2. That Project 1 grows from the previous quarter's work
3. That Project 2 involves multimedia
4. That students develop ownership of projects
5. That students spend a week with Ms. Johnson
6. That students develop skills and confidence with multimedia
7. That students be randomly regrouped
8. That each group designs its work plan
9. That I teach the rubric
10. That the groups do self-assessments
11. That formative feedback occurs
12. That class presentations occur
13. That adequate time is provided for group work
14. That students learn to be contributors to group work
15. That students produce quality multimedia projects

Significant Relationships

1. The relationship between 1 week with Ms. Johnson and student skills and confidence with multimedia
2. The relationship between group design of the work plans and group ownership of topic
3. The relationship between random regrouping and the development of group work plans
4. The relationship between group self-assessments and the provision of formative feedback
5. The relationship between formative feedback and learning how to contribute to meaningful cooperative work

---

research in our science classes. In the basic and natural sciences, it is actually possible to control for all relevant variables and consequently determine what causes what. However, in social science, this is never possible. When it comes to human behavior, results are influenced by such a wide array of variables that no one could ever control for every possible thing.

Fortunately, there are ways to enhance validity and reliability in social science research, and these will be elaborated on in Chapter 7.

- *Frame questions in a manner that is likely to make visible observable patterns and correlations between the presence of the independent variables and changes in the dependent variables* (e.g., What are the characteristics of teacher feedback that correspond to increases in the quality of student work?).

The answer to a question like this will help us recognize those specific teacher behaviors (feedback) that consistently accompany the student outcomes we're trying to influence.

Having completed the two-step walk-through of her theory, Ms. Pioneer was now ready to draft a set of research questions. These questions will become the heart of her inquiry. Ms. Pioneer's questions were as follows:

• What was the nature of the student performance on my two-priority achievement targets? (This question focuses on the two significant elements rated SU: *That students learn to be contributors to group work,* and *that students produce quality multimedia projects.*)

• How did the week with the media specialist influence student development of skills and their confidence with multimedia? (This question focuses on the first of the significant relationships rated SU: *The relationship of 1 week with Ms. Johnson and the development of student skills and confidence with multimedia.*)

• Which factors influenced the success of group work (e.g., assignment to groups, ownership of topic, quality of work plans, etc.)? And in what ways did those factors influence academic performance? (This question focuses on two of the other significant relationships rated SU: *The relationship of group design of the work plan to group ownership of topic and the relationship of random regrouping to the development of group work plans.*)

• What was the nature of the formative feedback provided by group self-assessment, and in what ways did it contribute to meaningful cooperative work? (This question focuses on the last two of the significant relationships rated SU: *The relationship of group self-assessments to the provision of formative feedback and the relationship of formative feedback to learning how to contribute to meaningful cooperative work.*)

It has often been noted that the most time-consuming aspect of the action research process is the work that leads up to the development of research questions. I have heard many first-time action researchers assert that it took them an entire year or more to come up with a good question. Look how well you did; it only took you six chapters!

Yes, sometimes we go through an extensive and lengthy process to find meaningful questions. However, if the questions that emerge end up directing you to information that will help you move ahead with your priorities, then the time invested should be considered well spent.

Ms. Pioneer can now look forward to the rest of the action research process knowing that everything she engages in from here on out will serve to better illuminate answers to the four questions she developed.

7

Building a
Data-Collection Plan

O n the surface, no aspect of the action research process appears more imposing than data collection. While the planning you've done up to this point has been time consuming, there is nothing new about that. Teachers already spend considerable time planning their instruction, units, and programs. While the work involved in Stages 1 and 2 of the action research process may be somewhat more extensive than what is required for other more routine types of planning, hopefully, the additional clarity and focus that was provided justified this expenditure of energy. At first glance, data collection doesn't usually seem as worthwhile.

Anticipating collecting data for action research, first-time researchers are most often worried about two things:

- The time required
- The need for precision

Because of the importance of these concerns, we begin our discussion on data collection by addressing each one separately.

■ DATA COLLECTION AND THE COMPETING DEMANDS FOR YOUR TIME

If finding the time for data collection means taking time away from other learning activities, the cost is greater than most dedicated teachers are willing to pay. Fortunately, this is not a choice you have to make. These two professional actions only appear to be in conflict if one holds a limited view of what constitutes teaching and what qualifies as data.

WHAT QUALIFIES AS TEACHING?   ■

As every teacher knows, there is more than one way to produce learning.

One mechanism educators have historically used for stimulating student learning is direct instruction, where the teacher positions himself or herself in front of the learner and demonstrates or tells the student how to accomplish a task, providing immediate feedback as the students practice the new skill or recite the new information. There can be much to commend this approach, especially with certain types of straightforward basic skill content. And many teachers have found that the direct instruction approach works well with learners that need consistent and immediate oversight. However, many teachers have also found that there are an even greater number of circumstances when direct instruction is not the best pedagogy. Many times, a reliance on direct instruction comes at a heavy cost: It is an all-consuming task, leaving little time and energy for monitoring, assessing, and adjusting.

More frequently, we serve our students and ourselves best when we become the *facilitators* of student learning. The students' role is transformed; they become what Ted Sizer (1984) defined as *knowledge workers.* Every day, the knowledge workers get up and go to their workplace (your classroom) with the expectation that they are to fulfill their job descriptions, which is to do whatever is necessary to acquire new knowledge and develop greater skill. In this framework, our role becomes analogous to the supervisor's function in the adult workplace. Our job becomes supplying whatever is needed to help the workers complete their jobs successfully, in this case, the acquisition of knowledge and skill. In this relationship, the ultimate responsibility for learning becomes shared and no longer rests solely on the teacher's shoulders.

In the adult workplace, supervisors occasionally demonstrate new techniques, but they spend far more time observing the workers and providing feedback. Supervisors also engage in planning, gathering data on worker productivity, and then adjusting individual and group work plans accordingly. They attempt to monitor everything critical to the work at hand so they can knowledgably and purposefully intervene whenever necessary. Last and most important, when the supervisors' goal is increasing worker productivity, they implement practices and procedures that hopefully result in the workers being motivated to give the work their very best efforts.

We need to approach data collection in the spirit of the action researcher as the learning supervisor. Most of the data-collection strategies presented here can occur during the workday, while the students are simultaneously purposefully and actively engaged in their own learning. Properly implemented, most of these strategies will also provide encouragement, direction, and motivation for your learners.

WHAT QUALIFIES AS DATA?   ■

If you think of data as something artificial, something that only comes into existence if and when we decide to solicit it, then generating and collecting data becomes a job unto itself. This isn't a productive way for you to view data collection.

As teacher researchers, you are well served using an extremely broad definition of data. Much action research methodology has been heavily influenced by anthropology. The primary work of anthropologists is observing, documenting, and trying to understand human cultures that are different from their own. The strategy most often used by field anthropologists is direct immersion into the cultures they are studying. While doing their work, they try to take in everything encountered, from one-on-one discussions to social activities, to local rituals. Even mundane activities, such as eating habits and home decor, are considered data sources. When all these observations are taken together and analyzed through a sensitive and thoughtful lens, the data can illuminate the culture that was the focus of the study.

■ DATA IN DESCRIPTIVE RESEARCH

When we are conducting descriptive research, our work is nearly identical to that of anthropologists. Just as they hope to understand what is going on in other cultures, unearthing the meaning of the behavior habits and beliefs demonstrated by the members of that culture, the descriptive action researcher is trying to understand the particular circumstances, norms of behavior, and meanings attached to the behavior by the participants in a specific school, classroom, or academic setting. For this reason, when we are engaging in descriptive action research, nearly everything that occurs in the setting we're studying has the potential to be meaningful data for understanding the following questions:

- What is going on here?
- Why is it happening?
- What impact is it having?

■ DATA IN QUASI-EXPERIMENTAL RESEARCH

Action researchers conducting quasi-experimental studies will also be well served to view data collection through the anthropologists' lens. Undoubtedly, the quasi-experimental researcher will want to monitor changes in performance on their priority achievement targets and, therefore, will almost always be using some quantitative methods. But that is only part of the process. The quasi-experimental action researcher needs to understand more than simply whether or not the priority targets were hit. It is equally, if not more important to understand

- Why the target was hit or missed
- How various elements of the theory of action contributed to success or failure
- What could be learned from this undertaking that might help illuminate other related aspects of the teaching-learning process

To address these issues, the quasi-experimental researcher has the same need as the descriptive researcher to deeply understand the context and the nuances of the environment where the action took place.

I can hear some of you asking, "Is he crazy? Did he say I ought to be acting as an anthropologist and collecting data on *everything* going on in my school or classroom?"

Not to worry. While it is true that the range of things that you may want data on is vast, the good news is that most of that data is already being and will continue to be collected, whether or not you ever decide to conduct action research.

One of our primary tasks as action researchers is finding *efficient* ways to collect and compile data that may already be out there. But before we examine ways to accomplish this, we should spend a few minutes considering the other big concern regarding data collection: achieving adequate precision.

DATA COLLECTION AND ∎
CONCERNS ABOUT PRECISION

It is unwise to collect flawed data and even worse to make use of it. None of us wants physicians making treatment decisions based on faulty data, nor do we want to fly in aircraft designed by engineers who relied on inaccurate information. Equally important, none of us wants our students to receive inadequate instruction simply because bad data suggested an unwise strategy. Even those of us with the most minimal backgrounds in research and statistics probably recall from Ed Psych 101 the two key conditions that must be met if data is to be used: validity and reliability.

- *Validity* refers to whether the data actually reflect the phenomena they claim to. For example, we would all agree that a measuring tape is a valid way to measure height and a scale is a valid mechanism for determining weight.

- *Reliability* refers to the accuracy of data. For example, even though a scale is a valid way to measure weight, any particular scale could be broken and consequently give an unreliable report on the weight of an object.

As professionals we want the data that we are using to influence our decisions on teaching and learning to be both valid and reliable. While there are a number of techniques researchers use to establish validity and reliability, the strategy used most frequently by action researchers is called *triangulation*. As pointed out earlier, triangulation is the strategy used by trial lawyers to prove a case beyond a reasonable doubt. In planning their cases, lawyers strive to have corroboration for every bit of testimony or evidence. Corroboration is accomplished by presenting additional independent pieces of evidence that lead to the same conclusion. While any single bit of evidence might be flawed or so imprecise that it could and should raise suspicion, when enough separate and independent pieces of data all point in the same direction, the credibility of the conclusion becomes apparent. Figure 7.1 gives an example of a *triangulation matrix*. The left column is where we place our research

Figure 7.1   Triangulation Matrix

Research Question	Data Source 1	Data Source 2	Data Source 3

SOURCE: Reprinted from Sagor (1993) with permission.

questions. Then, like a trial lawyer preparing a case, we consider all the independent sources of data that might be collected and presented so that when taken together, they will provide a credible answer to the question.

As we proceed through this chapter, you can use the triangulation matrix to increase the likelihood that the findings and conclusions that emerge from your research will have validity and reliability.

■ FISHING IN A SEA OF DATA

Schools and classrooms are data-rich environments. In any situation where life exists, data is continuously being created by what people choose to do and what they elect not to do. It involves who is doing the action and what they are doing as well as any explanations for why it is being done. In places where work is undertaken, such as schools, even more data is produced. When people work, they produce products; those products are data. Here are just a few of the work products typically created in schools that can also be used as sources of data:

Work Product	Data Regarding
Lesson plans	What I intend to teach
Grade book	The scores earned by my students
Attendance book	Who was and was not present
Faculty meeting agendas	The scope of a faculty business
PTA attendance	Parental interest in the PTA's work

Such a list could go on endlessly. The point is simply this: data is swirling around the schoolhouse, and this data relates to nearly everything that goes on inside it. Collecting this data is much like catching fish with a net. If a fine enough net is cast, it catches every living organism in the vicinity. We could cast such a net in our classrooms and potentially catch every minute thing that transpires inside, but the time it would take to sift through all that data, separating that which we value from that which is mostly irrelevant, will likely take more time than we have available.

The fisherman solves this problem by designing a net that allows undesirable items to flow through and that hopefully catches only that which was intended. This is analogous to the task before us as we make a plan for data collection.

■ SECURING RESEARCH ASSISTANTS

This chapter began with a discussion regarding the time issue. Frequently, the way professors and other research scientists deal with limitations on their time is by hiring research assistants, generally abbreviated as RA's. In grant-supported research teams, the individual responsible for the study is known as the PI, or principal investigator. In most cases, RA's are highly motivated graduate students who willingly do the grunt work of data collection for the privilege of working alongside the PI. So, you might be asking, where are you, the poorly paid and overworked teacher, conducting unfunded action research, going to find the motivated RA's to help you with your data collection? Fear not; the solution is nearer than you might think.

Earlier we touched on the difference between providing direct instruction and facilitating learning. We mentioned that when the teacher becomes the facilitator of learning and the students act as knowledge workers, they share the responsibility and accountability for the achievement of results.

Research in adult work settings has clearly established (Depree, 1998; Hersey & Blanchard, 1993) that when workers systematically monitor their own progress and self-assess their own work, performance improves. Even more important, when workers are delegated responsibility for monitoring their own work, they tend to hold themselves accountable to higher standards and show more pride in their ultimate accomplishments. So when we ask our students to become the primary collectors of data (the RA's) on their own learning and the activities they are engaged in, we are setting ourselves up for a classic win-win situation.

I would wager that you already know through personal experience that having your students compile portfolios, self-assess their work, maintain logs and journals (on their learning activities), and prepare their own student-led parent conferences is anything but a waste of time. By having the students monitor their own work, we help them learn and internalize what constitutes productive work as well as gain insight into how they learn best (the skill of meta-cognition).

It would be nice if I could say that by turning your students into RA's, you will free yourself from all data-collection duties. But that isn't the case. Having RA's on staff doesn't eliminate the participation of the lead scientist in the data-collection process, but it does transform the work of the PI. As the lead researcher, the PI's job begins with fleshing out the theory (what you did in Chapters 4 and 5), determining the research questions (what you did in Chapter 6), and creating a research design: determining what data is to be collected, who will collect it, when it will be collected, and how it will be analyzed. Those are the tasks we will concern ourselves with for the remainder of this chapter. As we proceed to build our research designs, our primary focus will be on strategies that

- Emphasize the use of *available data*
- Emphasize data that can be collected *while the teacher is facilitating learning*
- Maximize the value for students of *monitoring their own work*

BUILDING A TRIANGULATED DATA-COLLECTION PLAN ■

There are no limits to the variety of things that qualify as data or the techniques that action researchers can use to collect data. There is, however, a limit to how much can be covered in one book. For this reason, we will work through the process of building a triangulated data-collection plan with a few sample strategies that are frequently used and can be efficiently implemented by school-based action researchers. To illustrate, we make use once again of Ms. Pioneer's action research project.

During the first 9 weeks of this school year, Ms. Pioneer became deeply concerned about a particular problematic student, Joann Heathrow. Joann was diagnosed as ADHD and had a history of low academic performance tracing back to her first years in school. Despite medication, her off-task behavior and academic

Figure 7.2   Triangulation Matrix: Three ACR Questions

Research Question	Data Source 1	Data Source 2	Data Source 3
What did we actually do?			
What changes occurred with our priority achievement targets?			
What was the relationship between the actions taken and changes in performance on the achievement targets?			

Copyright © 2005 Corwin Press. All rights reserved. Reprinted from *The Action Research Handbook: A Four-Step Process for Educators and School Teams,* by Richard Sagor. Thousand Oaks, CA: Corwin Press, www.corwinpress.com. Reproduction authorized only for the local school site that has purchased this book.

problems continued unabated during the first quarter, and whenever the class engaged in cooperative activities, Ms. Pioneer noticed that Joann was off-task and frequently disruptive. Ms. Pioneer was at a loss as to what to do. She decided that since she didn't fully understand what was going on with Joann, she would conduct a descriptive action research study on Joann's experience in class. She chose social studies as the setting for her study, as the use of cooperative learning would likely prove problematic for Joann. She felt that if she could understand what was happening with Joann during second-quarter social studies, she might gain valuable insights into how to better meet her educational needs. She decided to frame her inquiry around the three ACR questions discussed in Chapter 6. Figure 7.2 is a triangulation matrix set up for use with the ACR questions.

The process of constructing a data-collection plan begins by taking one research question at a time and then asking this question:

> What is a source of data that could be *efficiently* collected that would provide good information to help answer this question?

After surfacing an initial answer, the process calls for continued brainstorming by repeatedly asking, *What is another source? And then another? And then another?* This process continues until the researcher believes that taken together, the multiple sources of data identified could provide a comprehensive, credible, valid, and reliable answer to the research question.

Ms. Pioneer began this process with a personalized version of *ACR Question 1: What exactly did the class and Joann do?*

She started by considering sources of data that were already available. She recognized that her plan book, weekly annotated to reflect what she actually taught, was one source of data. She realized that by cross-referencing Joann's *attendance records* with her plan book, she could determine what specific activities Joann experienced, and this would be a second data source. As her brainstorming continued, it occurred to her that since all of her students are required to keep their daily work in a portfolio, Joann's *daily work* could serve as a third source of data.

At this point she paused and asked herself, Will this be enough to create a credible report in answer to this question? She responded with a yes: A record of what was going on every day Joann was in attendance—as well as what she missed on the days she was absent, triangulated with the work she completed and failed to complete when she was there—would provide adequate information to answer the first ACR question.

She then moved to *Question 2: What changes occurred on my priority achievement targets?* Once again Ms. Pioneer began her brainstorming with readily available information. The first thing that came to mind was *her grade book*. This is a treasure trove of data as this is where she records grades on assignments, quizzes, tests, projects, and student journals. She then added Joann's *daily work folder* to her list of data sources. (Note: A single data source can help to answer multiple questions. For example, Joann's daily work folder can help answer both Questions 1 and 2.) Her thinking then shifted to include data she could collect during class while engaged in facilitating learning. She remembered that she regularly writes notes to herself on her personal digital assistant (PDA) while walking around the classroom.

She realized her *observational notes on Joann's behavior* would be data as well as the *comments she wrote on Joann's assignments.* Remembering that she required all her students to *self-assess their major assignments,* she added that to her list of data sources. Last, since one of her priority achievement targets was increased productive engagement during group work, she developed a rating scale that could be used each Friday to record a *weekly teacher rating of engagement.* The students could use this same rating scale to create a *weekly student rating of engagement.*

Once again it was time for Ms. Pioneer to stop and consider if, when taken together, the multiple sources of data she brainstormed would be adequate. She looked at her list asking, Will an examination of the information in *my grade book,* Joann's daily work, *my written notes* on Joann's behavior, *my comments on her papers,* her *self-assessments of her work,* and a comparison of Joann's and my *weekly engagement ratings* give me a good enough picture of changes in Joann's performance? While one can always collect more information, she was satisfied that the picture that would likely emerge from this data should illustrate most of the pertinent changes occurring in Joann's performance.

Now she moved to the final action research question: *What was the relationship between what was done and any changes noted in Joann's behavior?*

It immediately struck her that the data she would be using to answer the first two questions would also assist her in answering this last question. Specifically, she realized that looking at the activities engaged in (her plan book and Joann's attendance) and comparing them to what was accomplished (Joann's work, her grade book, her written comments on Joann's work, Joann's self-assessments, her anecdotal notes, and both student and teacher ratings) would enable her to find patterns that exist between certain classroom activities and Joann's performance. In the next chapter, when the focus shifts to analysis, a process for tracking the relationship between actions and outcomes will be presented.

Figure 7.3 shows Ms. Pioneer's completed triangulation matrix for the descriptive study on Joann Heathrow's second-quarter experience in Fifth Grade Social Studies.

Figure 7.3   Triangulation Matrix: Complete

Research Question	Data Source 1	Data Source 2	Data Source 3
What did we actually do?	• Lesson plan book	• Attendance record	• Joann's portfolio of daily work
What changes occurred with our priority achievement targets?	• Grade book (quizzes, homework, journals, reflection papers, projects, tests, weekly assessments)	• Observational notes • Comments on her tests and papers	• Joann's portfolio of daily work • Joann's self-assessments
What was the relationship between the actions taken and changes in performance on the achievement targets?	• Contrast lesson plans with performance data from grade book.	• Correlate lesson plans with observation notes. • Correlate lesson plans with comments on papers.	• Correlate lesson plans with material in Joann's portfolio. • Correlate lesson plans with Joann's self-assessments.

Now it's your turn. Using the blank triangulation matrix (Figure 7.4), start developing a viable data-collection plan with promise for producing the insights you will need to answer *your* action research questions.

Although each of the data-collection strategies Ms. Pioneer planned to use involved data that was either already being collected or could easily be collected while teaching, the amount of work involved in pulling all of this together could still be significant. Earlier it was mentioned that one way to manage the data-collection workload is by enlisting your students as research assistants. That will certainly help. But there are other efficiencies (both high and low tech) that can help you manage the work of data collection. We conclude this chapter and our work on Stage 3 of the action research process with a look at how technology can help you manage your work while implementing your theory of action and collecting the data you need to answer your research questions.

■ INTEGRATING EFFICIENCIES INTO YOUR DATA-COLLECTION WORK

Ms. Pioneer's data-collection plan made use of several sources of written material that are routinely produced in classrooms:

- The comments she wrote on Joann's papers
- Notes she wrote to herself when walking around the classroom
- Notes she might occasionally send to Joann's parents, the special ed teacher, and the school administrators regarding Joann
- Joann's self-assessments

Figure 7.4   Triangulation Worksheet

Research Question	Data Source 1	Data Source 2	Data Source 3

Copyright © 2005 Corwin Press. All rights reserved. Reprinted from *The Action Research Handbook: A Four-Step Process for Educators and School Teams,* by Richard Sagor. Thousand Oaks, CA: Corwin Press, www.corwinpress.com. Reproduction authorized only for the local school site that has purchased this book.

Compiling and organizing this data can become a project itself, however. One low-tech strategy I've used to tackle this problem involves the use of sets of carbonless paper.

Keeping File Copies of Narrative Data

Figure 7.5 is an example of a form I had printed on two-part carbonless paper (any commercial or district print shop is able to print on carbonless paper).

Whenever I write something to a student, including comments I would normally have written on his or her tests or on an assignment prior to returning it, I do so on the carbonless paper. Then I give the top sheet to the student or staple it to the paper and keep the yellow copy for my own records. If I am writing a note regarding a student to a parent, to another teacher, or to myself, I use the same paper. I keep a folder for each student, and at the end of the day, I simply drop my yellow copies of all the notes I've written into the appropriate folder, always making sure that each note is dated. If I never have reason to review these notes, nothing is lost. After all, it took hardly any time to file them. But should I ever need them as data for my action research, to prepare for a parent conference, or just to refresh my memory regarding what transpired with a student, simply opening the file and placing the notes in chronological order provides me with an easy way to review any patterns in what I've observed, be it regarding behavior or performance.

Keeping Running Records of Behavioral Ratings

In Chapter 3, we developed rating scales for measuring changes in performance on our achievement targets (the dependent variables). Earlier in this chapter, we discussed having students become RA's for our action research. Having students keep running records on their performance as measured on teacher-created rating scales is one excellent way to do this. This is especially powerful because of the motivational impact that students experience upon seeing a direct relationship between their efforts and the results obtained. It is no surprise that fitness buffs, weight watchers, and bridge players all keep running records of their results. Observing patterns of behavior change motivates people to keep trying, or conversely, it can provide the motivation for changing old habits.

Action researchers can effectively and efficiently turn students into RA's by first teaching them the use of the appropriate rating scales. When working with younger children, this can mean translating the scales you developed in Chapter 3 into "kid language" and providing each student with a copy or placing it on a poster on the wall of your room. With prereaders, teachers often do this by creating a scale with a range of smiley to frowney faces. You recall that Ms. Pioneer was hoping to see high levels of engagement from her students, so she developed a rating scale (Figure 7.6) for use in assessing this performance. She also wanted her students to contribute meaningfully to group work, so she created another rating scale for use in assessing cooperation (Figure 7.7).

Then, on a weekly basis, she asked the students to rate themselves using these two scales. Had she wanted more sensitive tracking, she could have requested daily ratings. This is another instance where I have found carbonless paper to be extremely helpful. Figure 7.8 is an example of a form I have students use for providing daily or weekly self-assessments. Ms. Pioneer could have had her students use forms such as these to make their weekly assessments.

Figure 7.5   Carbonless Paper

A note from the teacher . . .

Copyright © 2005 Corwin Press. All rights reserved. Reprinted from *The Action Research Handbook: A Four-Step Process for Educators and School Teams,* by Richard Sagor. Thousand Oaks, CA: Corwin Press, www .corwinpress.com. Reproduction authorized only for the local school site that has purchased this book.

Figure 7.6 Rating Scale: Engagement

Low		Basic		Developing	Meeting Expectations		Productive		High
The student didn't disrupt and interfere with others' learning.		The student did some of the assigned work. Worked productively for much of the period.		The student completed most of the assigned work. Worked productively for most of the period.	The student completed all of the assigned work. Was on task for the entire class period.		The student was on task for the entire period, completed all the assigned work, and went beyond expectations.		Student was on task the entire period and put forth a maximum effort.
1	2	3	4	5	6	7	8	9	10

Figure 7.7 Rating Scale: Cooperation

Low	Basic	Developing	Meeting Expectations	Productive	High
The student didn't disrupt and interfere with others' learning.	When prodded, the student made a contribution to group work.	The student contributed to group work. The student's labor moved the project forward.	The student made a unique, productive contribution to group work (something that would not have occurred if the student wasn't there).	The student took initiative to make the group more successful. Showed enthusiasm for the team and put forth a significant effort.	The student took initiative to make the group more successful. Showed enthusiasm for the team and put forth a significant effort. The student took affirmative steps to solicit and support the initiative of other group members.
1 2	3 4	5	6 7	8 9	10

Figure 7.8   Feedback Report

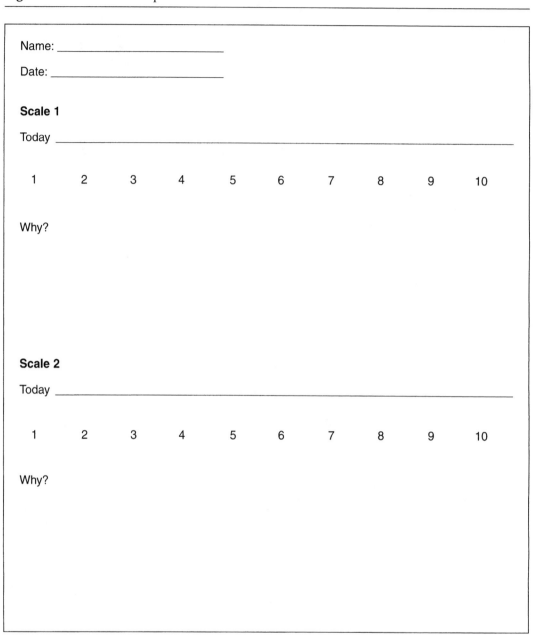

Copyright © 2005 Corwin Press. All rights reserved. Reprinted from *The Action Research Handbook: A Four-Step Process for Educators and School Teams,* by Richard Sagor. Thousand Oaks, CA: Corwin Press, www.corwinpress.com. Reproduction authorized only for the local school site that has purchased this book.

After each week's assessment, the students are asked to keep the top copy in their folders and drop the yellow copy into a box on my desk. This way I have a running record of how they saw themselves performing on my priority targets, and I can correlate those perceptions to what was occurring in class (there will be more specificity on establishing relationships between actions and performance in the next chapter, when we work on data analysis).

After a period of time, usually a number of weeks, I provide the students with another carbonless form (Figure 7.9), which they will use to produce a line graph reflecting their self-reports over this time period. These line graphs provide me with trend data for each of my students over an extended period. As a bonus, I am also able to effortlessly gather one additional piece of data, since once the students have graphed their performances, I will ask them to review their graphs and give me their explanations for any patterns or trends.

Again I have the students keep the original in their portfolios and provide a copy to me. This way my RA's do the work of compiling the trends, which saves me a lot of labor, and by doing it this way, I have provided them with a chance to take stock of, assume responsibility for, and explain to themselves their own choices of behavior.

To see the power and time saving of this one simple strategy, consider the following scenario. We'll assume I am doing action research with a class of 25 students, compiling daily ratings on two different scales over a 3-week period. This amounts to 30 assessments per student, 750 assessments per class. If I provide my students with 1 minute per day to jot down their daily ratings and then give them 15 minutes to complete the summaries at the close of the 3-week period, I will have had all this data compiled and summarized with an allocation of a mere 30 minutes of class time. Most important, this meager time investment provides an opportunity for my students to take ownership of their own improvement. (Resource A contains detailed instructions on the use of carbonless reporting forms for collecting and analyzing data.)

USING PERSONAL DIGITAL ASSISTANTS AND PERSONAL COMPUTERS TO COMPILE AND ASSEMBLE ACTION RESEARCH DATA

The beauty of the time-honored teacher grade book is that in this one easy-to-carry document, a host of different types of information regarding the performance of each of our students can be compiled. In one set of columns, we have attendance data; on another page we have a record of their homework as well as quiz grades and major assignments. And the list goes on. Data input is easy. When taking roll, we simply check if the student is present or absent, and before we return papers, we jot down the grade we assigned. Of course, pulling all this together (adding up each column and figuring the averages) can take considerable time at the end of the grading period.

Nowadays it is a rare computer that doesn't come delivered with a spreadsheet program already installed. And if you don't own spreadsheet software, it is easy to acquire. Basically, a spreadsheet is simply a grade book with an unlimited number of expandable columns. However, it is better than a hard-copy grade book in three big ways:

1. It will automatically compile statistics (e.g., average the scores in each column), making end-of-term grading easier.

2. The cells of the spreadsheet can expand infinitely. In our grade books, each cell is just a fraction of an inch wide, not providing too much room for data. But in a spreadsheet you can write an entire note or comment, even copy a photograph or a scanned image of student work into a single cell.

3. Last, with a spreadsheet you can easily compute averages for subgroups, allowing for disaggregation by gender, ethnicity, past performance, and so forth, on virtually any assignment. This is extremely helpful when you are conducting data analysis, which is discussed in the next chapter.

Figure 7.9 Feedback Summary

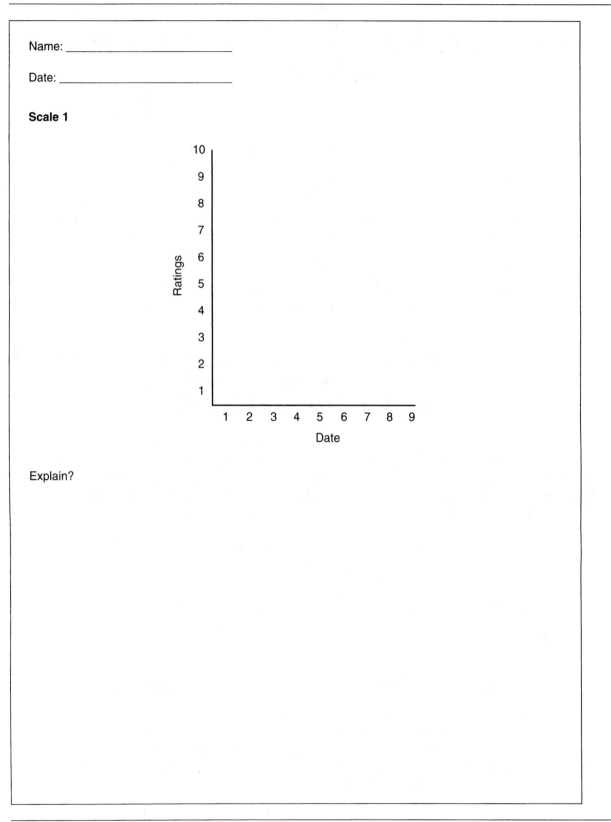

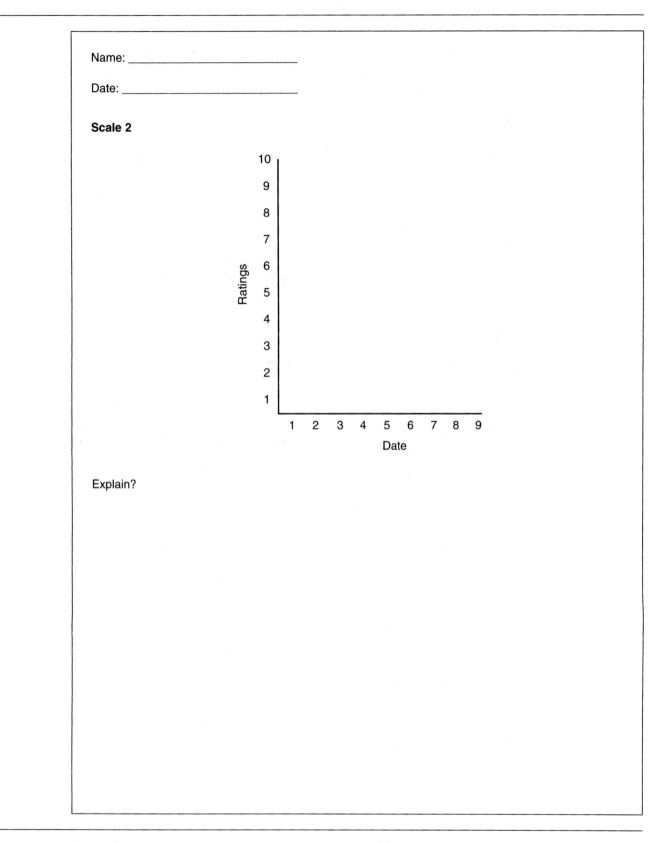

Name: _____

Date: _____

Scale 2

Explain?

Copyright © 2005 Corwin Press. All rights reserved. Reprinted from *The Action Research Handbook: A Four-Step Process for Educators and School Teams,* by Richard Sagor. Thousand Oaks, CA: Corwin Press, www.corwinpress.com. Reproduction authorized only for the local school site that has purchased this book.

But perhaps the best thing about using a spreadsheet as your electronic grade book is its portability. When using a handheld PDA or a tablet PC, teachers can input data as they walk around the room. Tablet PC's, PDA's, and computerized writing pads now allow teachers to write long-hand notes or score student work and then have them automatically converted into print for placement in their computerized grade book. With voice recognition software, teachers are even able to dictate notes into a digital recorder or microphone and have their comments turned into text.

What enables doctors to provide personalized treatment for each one of their diverse patients is having a readily accessible running record of all the pertinent data on each patient's condition. Of course, the doctor has a support staff, which transcribes the doctor's notes, inputs lab data, and places the various items into the correct file. It is unlikely that we will see that type of support provided to teachers in the near future. But fortunately, spreadsheets and portable computing technology can do nearly the same thing for the overworked classroom teacher.

This brings us nearly to the close of our discussion on Stage 3 of the action research process. It is now time for you, the action researcher, to begin the fun stuff: implementing your theory of action and collecting the data as indicated in your triangulated data-collection plan. There is only one little task that needs to be discussed before you commence action on your theory.

■ KEEPING A RESEARCHER'S JOURNAL

I strongly suggest that during this upcoming period of implementation, you keep a researcher's journal. Needless to say, the more observations you collect in your journal, the more information you will have available when you arrive at the final stage of the process. Even if your data-collection plan doesn't call for using information from a teacher's journal and/or if journaling isn't something you are comfortable doing, keeping a researcher's journal isn't a big project and takes very little time. In fact, you needn't even write in your researcher's journal on a regular basis. What is important, however, is to make notes in your journal whenever you elect to depart from your stated theory of action. When this happens, in your note you should indicate the date, the specific actions that differed from your original theory, and the rationale for making these adjustments.

As a teacher researcher, your first and most sacred duty is to the first part of your title, your work as *a teacher*. Because that is your most important job, you should always feel comfortable deviating from your enunciated theory of action wherever and whenever you think it is in your students' interest. However, later, when you put on your researcher hat, it will become essential to document what actually transpired and the rationale for adjustments in your theory of action. Unless you have a record of what was actually done and why, you will be unable to learn from your experience.

Keep in mind, often the best learning comes from serendipity. You should stay open to letting this happen. Your researcher's journal will allow you to understand the significance of unanticipated events as well as enable you to share this learning with others.

The data-collection sources discussed in this chapter are simply examples. You are encouraged to use them to stir your imagination, while keeping in mind that there are virtually unlimited data-selection strategies available to you as a creative action researcher.

8

Analyzing the Data

We are now ready to begin our work on the final stage of the action research process, Stage 4: Reflecting on Data and Planning Informed Action. There are three distinct activities that occur during this stage:

- Analyzing
- Planning
- Reporting

The process begins by *analyzing* the data that's been collected. Then the insights gained from that analysis are used to prepare a *plan of action*. This is followed by *reporting and sharing* what was learned with colleagues. In this chapter, we focus on the first of those activities, analyzing the action research data. In the next two chapters, the focus will shift to strategies for action planning and reporting.

Every action research project is a story of what transpired during the course of the research. As in the world of literature, each story has its own theme, plot, and set of characters. Our stories can range from a report on a single student's experience in one of our classes to the story of what was learned while teaching familiar content in a new way, or it could be the saga of a faculty and its attempt to become more collegial. Now that we have arrived at Stage 4, the events of your story have already occurred. Every element (the characters, conflicts, setting, and themes) can be understood through your data. The task before you, when engaged in data analysis, is to figure out a way to liberate the story that is currently lying dormant inside your data and give it an opportunity to take form and reveal itself. In this chapter, we review several ways to accomplish this.

Just as the nature of your research questions influenced the types of data collected, the nature of that data influences the strategy you will use for analysis. When you prepared your research design (Chapter 7), we discussed the use of a set of three generic ACR research questions and how effective they can be with a wide range of research foci. Let's now examine a few generic approaches to data analysis, which can effectively bring to the surface the stories residing in most sets of school data. The first approach is called a *trend analysis.* This is a versatile strategy that can easily be modified and adjusted for use with an array of data sources and should help you answer a broad range of action research questions.

■ TREND ANALYSIS

Above all, education is about growth and development. Students, classes, and schools change over time. When things are proceeding as we'd like, the direction of those changes is positive. As educators, our hope and professional assumption is that the longer someone is engaged in the educational process, the greater will be his or her development. In this book, we framed our rationale for engaging in action research as a mechanism to help us find the best routes for fostering that development, and to assist us as professionals in documenting our own growth as we traveled ever closer to our vision of universal success.

The specific areas of development you want to document are changes in performance on your priority achievement targets. When analyzing action research data, your goal is to accomplish two things:

- Tracing any and all changes in performance that occurred in the effort to reach your priority achievement targets
- Understanding whatever pertinent factors or circumstances contributed to those changes

Conceptually, the way action researchers usually approach the analysis of data is very similar to the way historians and other reporters of naturally occurring events approach theirs. What first attracts the attention of a historian or a reporter is the awareness of a compelling event. Whether that event is a conflict, a discovery, a scandal, an accident, or an election, the analysis process begins with the reporter (e.g., historian, researcher) becoming aware that something has happened that he or she wants to know more about. Invariably, the aspect of the event that made it noteworthy was that it was unique, or at the very least, significantly different than what had gone before. After an event has been initially reported, the focus switches to understanding the event. Having already *described* what occurred, historians train their eyes and ears backward, trying to understand *what contributed to* or otherwise influenced the event. The consuming questions at this point become

- Why did this occur?
- Why did it occur here and not elsewhere?
- Why did it happen now and not at some other time?

The events we action researchers want to report on are changes in performance on our priority achievement targets. The circumstances that led up to the events are the things that transpired as the learner, the class, or the program developed to its current level of performance. Our job when conducting data analysis is to use the data we have available to deepen our understanding regarding which of all the infinite number of things that transpired (the potential independent variables) actually influenced the changes in performance noted on the dependent variable.

Since change occurs over time, we can pictorially illustrate the analysis process as a line graph, such as that shown in Figure 8.1.

Figure 8.1 Trend Analysis

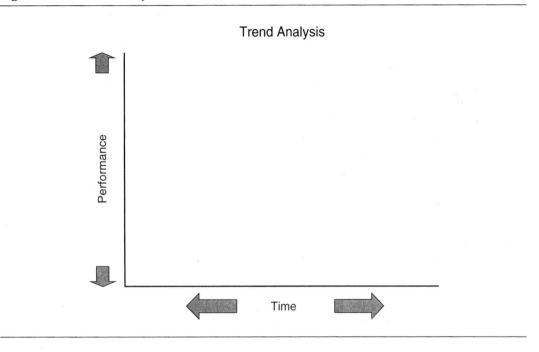

Figure 8.2 U.S. Highway Fatalities, 1988–98

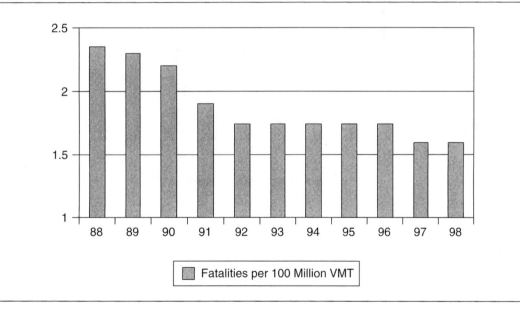

In Figure 8.1, the vertical axis represents performance on the achievement target and the horizontal axis represents the events that occurred over the term of the study.

Figure 8.2 is a graph representing the rates of highway fatalities in the United States from 1988 to 1998. An examination of this graph reveals something quite positive. Fatalities, per 100 million vehicle miles, dropped dramatically during this decade.

If you were working in the field of transportation safety and had as one of your achievement targets reducing automobile fatalities, you would be delighted by this trend in performance. In all likelihood, you and your colleagues would have been taking many different actions designed to reduce the fatality rate. At this point, you would have significant interest in determining which of those actions, if any, contributed to this positive change on this priority achievement target.

No doubt you and your colleagues would have been collecting data on several aspects of driver behavior, and you would now be interested in seeing if that data can help you understand what changes in behavior corresponded to the drop in fatalities. One of the sets of data you have available is the annual reports on the use of seat belts. Wondering if there might be a relationship between seat belt use and highway fatalities, you decide to contrast seat belt use from 1988 to 1998 with the fatality data. Figure 8.3 shows these two data sets side by side.

A cursory look at these graphs reveals a clear pattern: The decline in fatalities corresponds very closely with the increase in the use of seatbelts. Needless to say, you would want to do further analysis employing other sets of data before you claim to have demonstrated this relationship as an irrefutable fact, yet at this point it is beginning to appear that the actions you and your colleagues took to encourage seat belt use may well be paying dividends.

Figure 8.3   Reports on Seat Belts and Highway Fatalities

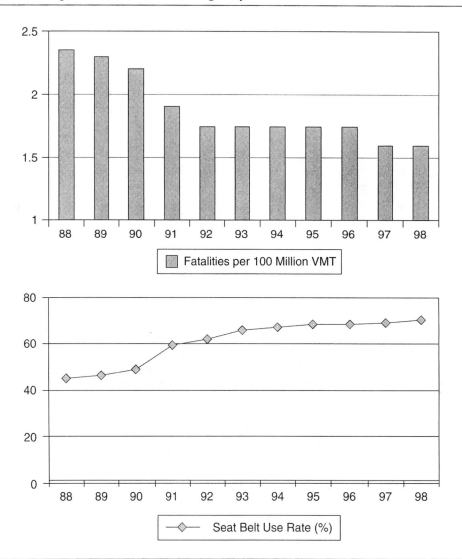

ORGANIZING DATA TO HELP ANSWER THE THREE GENERIC QUESTIONS ■

When conducting a trend analysis with the data collected in response to the three ACR research questions, it is helpful to compile and review the data in the same order as the questions. To see how this is done, let's return to Ms. Pioneer's descriptive study of Joann Heathrow's experience in her class.

ACR QUESTION 1: WHAT DID WE DO? ■

Any action researchers who took the time to detail their theories of action already have in their possession important historical documents containing data on what they *intended to do.* The priority pies and graphic reconstructions produced during Stage 2 provide accurate data on what was planned and what they intended to do as of the date these documents were created. Therefore, the first step of the process is to revisit the original theory of action and then review your data for evidence of four things:

1. Was the theory of action followed as written?

2. In what fashion was the theory of action implemented?

3. What, if any, elements of the theory were omitted or changed?

4. What, if any, significant actions were taken that were not part of the original theory?

There are several ways we can go about answering these questions. One is to examine the sum of our actions and determine the degree to which our investments of time and energy corresponded to the percentages we had anticipated and illustrated on our priority pies (see Chapter 4). A second strategy is to see if we faithfully followed through on the theory of action as detailed on our graphic reconstructions (see Chapter 5). If you used the Time Priority Tracking Form (Figure 6.2) and kept a researcher's journal or an annotated plan book (or both), you have all the data you need to answer ACR Question 1. The following three-step process can help you synthesize this data.

Step 1: Allocating Time

Using the worksheet provided (Figure 8.4), enter the data you collected on your Time Priority Tracking Forms.

The next step is to illustrate the time actually invested over the course of your study. This is done by creating a line graph. Figure 8.5 illustrates the ebb and flow of the time spent by Mr. Seeker when doing his action research on improving his student's writing of five-paragraph essays.

Now it is time to examine the *time allocation graph* by category to see if any notable patterns or outliers can be identified. For example, was there an extended period of time (perhaps an entire month) where nothing was done in a particular category of action, or was time spent on a category consistent throughout the project? When we look at Figure 8.5, we can see that Mr. Seeker spent significant time early in the course on mechanics and grammar, and the time he devoted to instruction on editing increased as the term progressed.

Figure 8.4 Summary Time Priority Sheets

Category of Action	Week 1	Week 2	Week 3	Week 4	Week 5	Week 6	Week 7	Week 8	Week 9	Totals
Totals:										

Copyright © 2005 Corwin Press. All rights reserved. Reprinted from *The Action Research Handbook: A Four-Step Process for Educators and School Teams*, by Richard Sagor. Thousand Oaks, CA: Corwin Press, www.corwinpress.com. Reproduction authorized only for the local school site that has purchased this book.

Figure 8.5 Time Use Graph: Eighth-Grade Writing in Hours

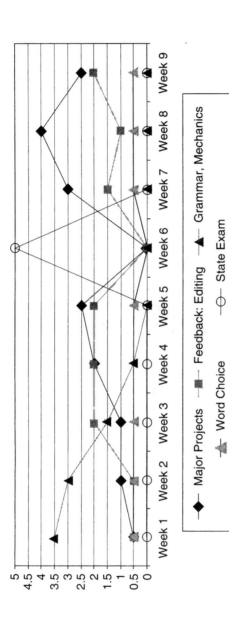

Category of Action	Week 1	Week 2	Week 3	Week 4	Week 5	Week 6	Week 7	Week 8	Week 9
Major projects	.5	1	1	2	2.5	0	3	4	2.5
Feedback: editing	.5	.5	2	2	2	0	1.5	1	2
Grammar, mechanics	3.5	3	1.5	.5	0	0	0	0	0
Word choice	.5	.5	.5	.5	.5	0	.5	.5	.5
State exam	0	0	0	0	0	5	0	0	0

You may want to use Figure 8.6 to plot the allocation of time across the categories of action illustrated on your original priority pie.

Another valuable use of the data on the summary sheet (Figure 8.4) is to determine if the actual allocation of time was consistent with what you had anticipated when planning your project. This is done by producing a grand total of the hours spent working on the project and then creating subtotals for each category of action. To calculate the percentage of time invested per category, divide each subtotal by the grand total. Then using these percentages, draw a pie graph illustrating the actual expenditure of time.

By placing the priority pie, constructed prior to commencing action, next to the pie graph you just produced, you will have produced a visual that clearly and succinctly contrasts your original theory on time allocation with the actual expenditure of your time. Figure 8.7 shows the two graphs produced by Mr. Seeker.

Now, taking all the data you compiled to answer ACR Question 1, it is time to summarize this data in clear, unambiguous, bulleted statements. For example, you might be able to write statements like the following:

- The project lasted for 18 weeks.
- Approximately 16% of class time was spent each week on journal writing (30 minutes per week).
- Overall, 30% of class time (an average of 3 hours per week) was spent engaged in work on major papers.
- Overall, 5% of class time was used for teacher feedback.
- Overall, 10% of class time was spent on group and peer feedback.
- Overall, 20% of class time was spent working on mechanics and grammar.
- During 6 weeks (3 in October, 2 in November, 1 in December), zero class time was spent on either drafting or revising major papers.

Step 2: Looking for Patterns

Read through your researcher's journal, your annotated lesson plans, or both with paper and pen in hand. Whenever you notice something that appears to be a pattern (an observation or activity that occurred three or more times), jot down a phrase that describes that pattern. For example, your list might contain items like the following:

- Class discussions re: grades
- Reviewing previously taught material
- Use of editing groups

Now reread the journal or go back through the annotated lesson plans and, using an analysis form like the one in Figure 8.8, note the date of the occurrence and tabulate the frequency of the occurrences by category.

Once again it is time to summarize this information as bulleted findings. Some examples follow of findings that classroom action researchers might identify:

- Class discussions were held following the return of each major writing assignment.

Figure 8.6 Trends in Time Use

Project: _____

Approximate Time Spent	Week 1	Week 2	Week 3	Week 4	Week 5	Week 6	Week 7	Week 8	Week 9
5 hours									
4.5 hours									
4 hours									
3.5 hours									
3 hours									
2.5 hours									
2 hours									
1.5 hours									
1 hour									
0.5 hour									

Copyright © 2005 Corwin Press. All rights reserved. Reprinted from *The Action Research Handbook: A Four-Step Process for Educators and School Teams*, by Richard Sagor. Thousand Oaks, CA: Corwin Press, www.corwinpress.com. Reproduction authorized only for the local school site that has purchased this book.

Figure 8.7 Anticipated and Actual Time Use

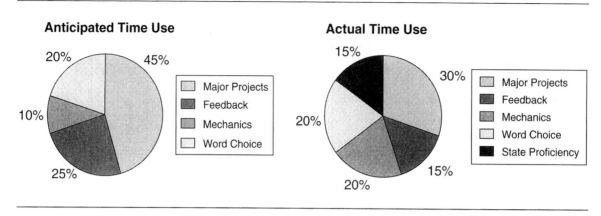

- On 7 occasions, I made note of the need to spend an entire class period reviewing previously taught material.
- On 4 of the 5 times that peer editing was used, it took at least twice the allocated time.

Step 3: Creating a Timeline

The purpose of this step is to help you construct the equivalent of the horizontal axis of the trend graph (see Figure 8.1) through the use of your teacher journal or annotated lesson plans. First, read through the plans or journal entries for each period of time (generally weekly) and then write a brief summary of the key actions that occurred during that week. Then write this out on a long sheet of chart paper. Figure 8.9 shows Ms. Pioneer's time line for second-quarter social studies.

Now review your time line as well as your sets of bulleted statements of findings and write a short narrative describing what was done by you and your students. A typical narrative might read something like the one written by Mr. Seeker:

> My theory of action called for spending nearly half (45%) of class time on major projects and 25% on feedback. In practice, less than a third (30%) of class time was spent on major projects and much less time than I had anticipated (15%) on feedback. Significantly, more time was spent with direct instruction on mechanics and grammar (20%) than the 10% that I had intended. Last, 15% of class time was used to prepare for and take the state proficiency exam, a category of action that I hadn't even considered when planning this class.

■ ACR QUESTION 2: WHAT CHANGES OCCURRED REGARDING THE ACHIEVEMENT TARGETS?

Using your grade book or whatever other records you've kept on achievement regarding your priority achievement targets over the term of the project, place the data in a

Figure 8.8 Activity Analysis Form

Step 1: Read through your log, journal, or annotated lesson plans for activities or events that appear to recur. Jot down a phrase that describes the recurring event in the left-hand column.

Step 2: Reread the documents, jotting down the date for each occurrence of particular events or activities and a descriptive comment if necessary.

Event or Activity	Dates of Occurrence	Frequency	Comments
Example: Current events journal writing	9/8, 9/15, 9/22, 9/29, 10/6, 10/13, 10/20, 10/27, 11/4	9 times; 1 per week	Occurs first 15 minutes of class every Monday

Copyright © 2005 Corwin Press. All rights reserved. Reprinted from *The Action Research Handbook: A Four-Step Process for Educators and School Teams*, by Richard Sagor. Thousand Oaks, CA: Corwin Press, www.corwinpress.com. Reproduction authorized only for the local school site that has purchased this book.

Figure 8.9 Ms. Pioneer's Instructional Timeline

Week 1	Week 2	Week 3	Week 4	Week 5	Week 6	Week 7	Week 8	Week 9
Students work in jigsaw groups. Groups brainstormed, discussed, and selected a topic. Constructed an outline. Groups assigned tasks based on the outline. Thursday spent in library. Groups organized note cards for presentations.	Groups developed presentations. Paired and did dress rehearsals of presentations with feedback. Thursday finalized the presentations. The first two groups presented their work.	Group presentations. On Friday groups met for 20 minutes to critique their own work. Class discussion on "What we learned by doing this project."	Orientation to the technology lab with Ms. Johnson, the media specialist.	Introduced the multimedia project by showing a mock-up produced by Ms. Johnson. Students regrouped. Tuesday was spent with team building. Groups selected a topic and made storyboards. Thursday and Friday in the computer lab working on group project.	No class on Monday due to the assembly. Working on the individual portions of the group project. Students could work in the classroom or computer lab.	The entire week was spent working as groups finalizing the multimedia project.	Monday and Tuesday in the auditorium: presentations of the multi-media projects. Students assessed individually and group consensus on the assessment. Teams gave feedback. Class party to celebrate. Preparing for the writing assessment.	Monday and Tuesday district writing assessment. Watched a film Wednesday and Thursday, and Friday was the field trip to the courthouse.

chronological sequence for an individual student or category of students, depending on the nature of your study. Figure 8.10 shows the grades earned during the second quarter by Joann, the hyperactive fifth-grade student in Ms. Pioneer's class. Ms. Pioneer recorded grades for homework, quizzes, journals, and group projects. She then used a line graph to ferret out any trends in this data on Joann's performance. Figure 8.11 reflects Joann's grades over the 9 weeks of second-quarter social studies.

The next step in a trend analysis is comparing and contrasting trends in performance to see if they might have been influenced by variables other than your actions. With classroom research, this is easily accomplished by graphing average

Figure 8.10   Joann's Grades

Week	Journals	Homework Completion	Reflection Papers	Quizzes	Group Project Grades
1	55	80		70	
2	60	60		60	
3	50	60	65	70	85
4		60		80	
5	75	80		90	
6	80	100		90	
7		80		100	
8	90	80	85	90	95
9	100	80		100	

Figure 8.11   Second-Quarter Social Studies Grades

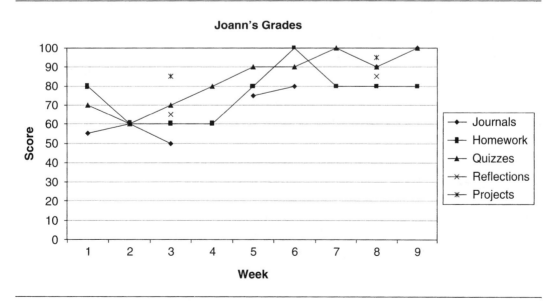

Figure 8.12   Comparison of Quiz Grades

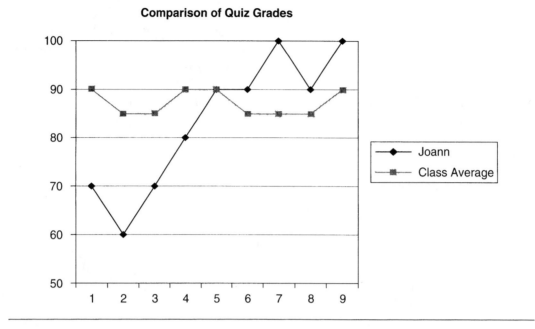

class (or subgroup) performance over the same time frame and comparing the achievement of individual students with overall class or subgroup performance. Figure 8.12 is an example of such a graph. It contrasts Joann's quiz grades with the average grades of her classmates.

Another illustration of this process can be found in Figure 8.13. This contrasts Joann's grades with her classmates' on each of the five categories of performance tracked in Ms. Pioneer's grade book.

Once you have graphed or otherwise summarized all the performance data you have collected, it is time to review this data and summarize them as bulleted findings. For example, Ms. Pioneer might write the following:

- During the first semester, the average homework completion rate for the class was 95% while Joann's homework completion rate was 77%.
- Joann's homework completion rate went from 65% the first 4 weeks to 85% in the last 4 weeks.
- The class average quiz grade was 87%; Joann's average quiz grade was 83%.
- Joann's quiz grades went from 70% the first 4 weeks, to 95% in the last 4 weeks.

■ DISAGGREGATION

Oftentimes we want to see if our actions had a differential impact based on certain background or behavioral characteristics of the participants. This is called disaggregation and is accomplished by subdividing performance data by any categories we suspect could be relevant. As a teacher you start this process by considering the different demographic subgroups represented by your students and then asking

Figure 8.13 Comparison of Second-Quarter Grades

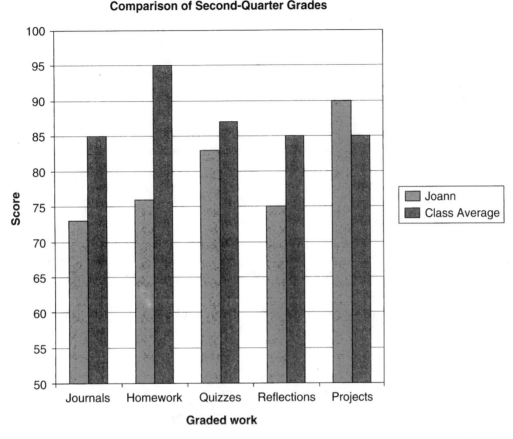

yourself if you suspect it would be worth contrasting performance across these groups. For example, many teachers have found it valuable to disaggregate their data by categories such as the following:

- Gender
- Past level of academic performance
- Ethnic group
- Primary home language
- Years in attendance at your school

Dr. Hernandez, the principal who was working on increasing faculty collegiality, might have found it valuable to disaggregate her data by grade level, departmental affiliation, years of teaching, years on the faculty, and so on. Often schoolwide action research teams find it helpful to compare the performance of students by both past performance (previous grades) and attendance history, say, contrasting those who attended district schools for 5 or more consecutive years with students who had attended local schools for less than 2 years.

Once you have disaggregated your data, compute and graph the averages for each of the subgroups you deemed relevant. Compare and contrast the performance of these groups and summarize all significant patterns as bulleted statements.

Figure 8.14   Monthly Collegiality Ratings

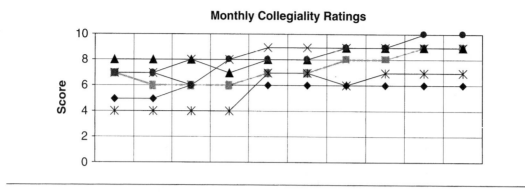

Figure 8.14 is a graph that compares average teacher ratings on Dr. Hernandez's collegiality rating scale across six different departments during the course of her project.

Form 8.15 has been provided for you to use for graphing the performance data you've collected.

Repeat the foregoing steps for each set of relevant performance data you have collected.

■ ACR QUESTION 3: WHAT WAS THE RELATIONSHIP BETWEEN ACTIONS TAKEN AND ANY CHANGES IN PERFORMANCE ON THE TARGETS?

You will need to do two things to answer this question. The first makes use of the findings you generated in answering the first two questions. Place the time line you developed (see Figure 8.9) when analyzing the data you collected in answer of Question 1 under the horizontal axis of the graph you created when analyzing the performance data in response to Question 2. This step is illustrated in Figure 8.16 using Ms. Pioneer's assessments and Joann's self-assessments for engagement during the 9-week quarter.

Ms. Pioneer actually has two sets of data, both of which rightfully belong on the horizontal axis. The first is the summary of her lessons (Figure 8.7); the other is the collection of weekly narrative comments she wrote regarding Joann's behavior. Figure 8.17 incorporates both of those sets of data on the same time line.

It is at this point that Ms. Pioneer should go back and look for changes in Joann's performance, either positive or negative, and look to see if there were any particular actions or activities that corresponded to those changes. The purpose here is to see if she can isolate a trend, such as the one between seat belt use and fatalities (see Figures 8.2 and 8.3) to help her explain the story of Joann's experience in class.

Let's return again to Mr. Seeker and his attempt to help his students write better five-paragraph persuasive essays. The graphs (Figures 8.18 and 8.19) reflect disaggregated data on the weekly self-report assessments by his students on the effort they expended. Figure 8.18 compares those students who had been average performers (previous year's GPAs of 2.00–2.9) with the low performers (GPA < 2.00) and

Figure 8.15 Performance Graph

Project: _____

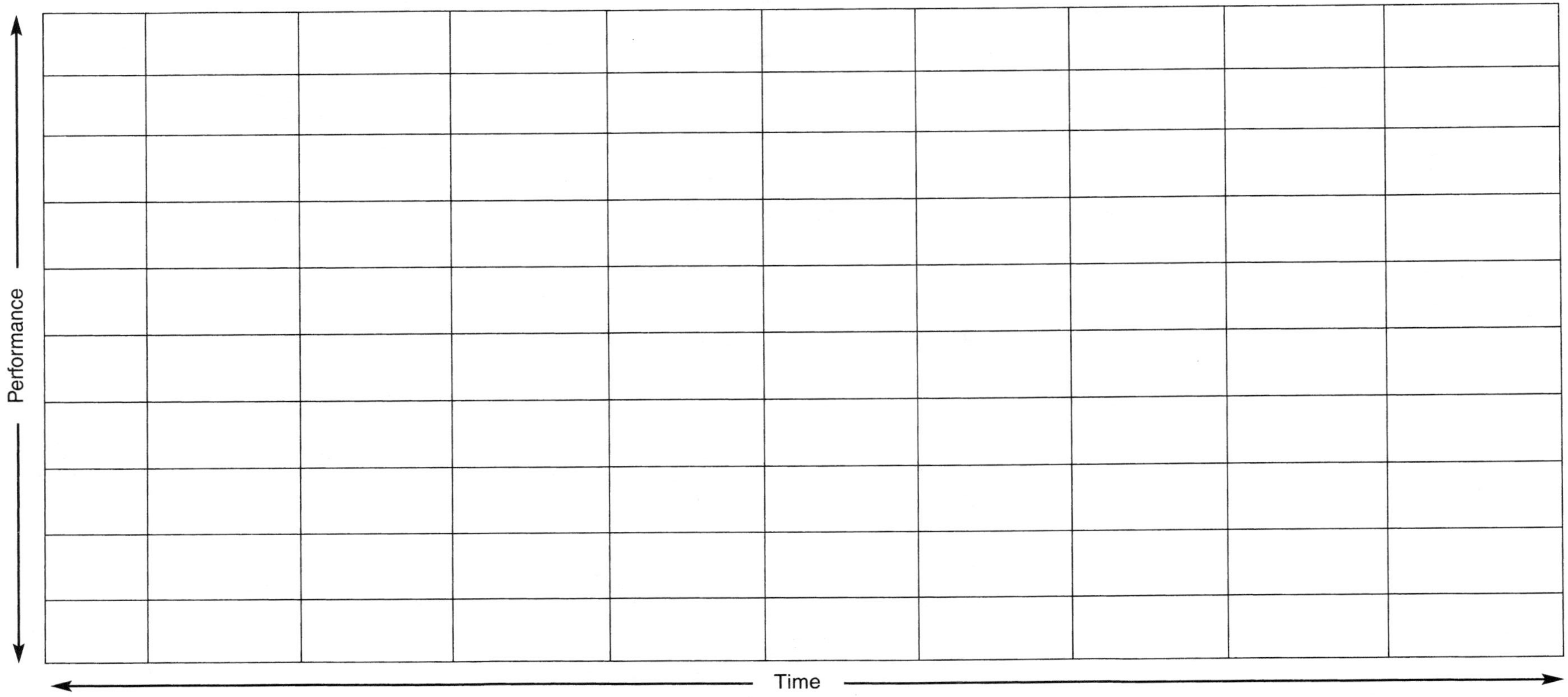

Performance

Time

Copyright © 2005 Corwin Press. All rights reserved. Reprinted from *The Action Research Handbook: A Four-Step Process for Educators and School Teams*, by Richard Sagor. Thousand Oaks, CA: Corwin Press, www.corwinpress.com. Reproduction authorized only for the local school site that has purchased this book.

Figure 8.16   Student and Teacher Ratings of Engagement

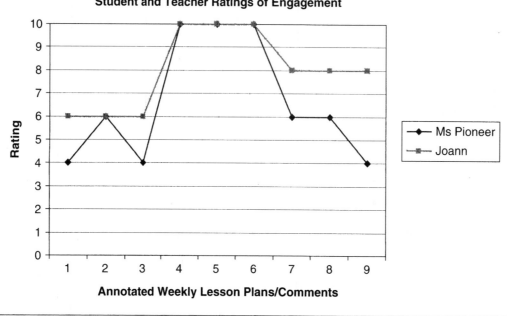

high performers (GPA > 3.00). Figure 8.19 contrasts this same class of Mr. Seeker's students, but this time, disaggregated by gender.

When Mr. Seeker examined these graphs, he could see that the effort expended by the middle and low performers began dropping during the second week of February and continued in this depressed state throughout the month of March. When he looked on the horizontal axis to see what, if any, events or actions corresponded with this drop in effort, it became apparent that when his regular writing program was suspended and the class focus shifted to preparation for the state test, the students reported putting forth less effort. Based on this analysis, Mr. Seeker could have noted the following regarding the achievement target of "effort":

- Average class performance declined during the period of preparation for the state exam.
- Average performance of the boys declined sharply during the period of preparation for the state exam.
- The average performance of the average- and low-performing students declined during the period of preparation for the state exam.
- There was no significant change in performance of the high-achieving students during the period of preparation for the state exam.
- There was a slight improvement in performance of the girls during the period of preparation for the state exam.

It is now time for you to look for changes in performance reflected in your data and see if you can identify a pattern or patterns of corresponding actions or events that might help explain these changes. Jot down in narrative bulleted form any changes in performance and any significant corresponding events.

Figure 8.17 Instructional Timeline

Week 1	Week 2	Week 3	Week 4	Week 5	Week 6	Week 7	Week 8	Week 9
Students work in jigsaw groups. Groups brainstormed, discussed, and selected a topic. Constructed an outline. Groups assigned tasks based on the outline. Thursday spent in library. Groups organized note cards for presentations.	Groups developed presentations. Paired and did dress rehearsals of presentations with feedback. Thursday finalized the presentations. The first two groups presented their work.	Group presentations. On Friday groups met for 20 minutes to critique their own work. Class discussion on "What we learned by doing this project."	Orientation to the technology lab with Ms. Johnson, the media specialist.	Introduced the multi-media project by showing a mock-up produced by Ms. Johnson. Students regrouped. Tuesday was spent on team building. Groups selected a topic and made storyboards. Thursday and Friday in the computer lab working on group project.	No class on Monday due to the assembly. Working on the individual portions of the group project. Students could work in the classroom or computer lab.	The entire week was spent working as groups finalizing the multimedia project.	Monday and Tuesday in the auditorium: presentations of the multi-media projects. Students assessed individually and group consensus on the assessment.	Monday and Tuesday district writing assessment. Watched a film Wednesday and Thursday, and Friday was the field trip to the courthouse.
Joann seemed disinterested and appeared to be off task most of the week. She appeared busy when we were in the library, but I'm not sure she was doing the assigned work. I had to stay on her all period Friday.	Joann was far more engaged this week than last. She seemed to take ownership of her group's work. She even showed some leadership. Later in the week she needed prodding to stay on task.	I had trouble with Joann this entire week! She refused to attend when other students were presenting. Ultimately, I had her sit with me, just to keep her from disrupting.	I think the computer is Joann's thing. She was excited the moment we entered the lab. A few times I had to ask her to curb her enthusiasm as she occasionally took over for Ms. Johnson. I had to remind her it wasn't her class.	Joann assumed the role of group leader this week. At first I thought the other kids would object to her bossy style, but they seemed to genuinely value her expertise with technology. What pleased me was that she stayed on task and focused on the assigned work!	I'm glad she was absent Monday. She would have had real trouble sitting still at the assembly. It was another good week in class. Joann acted as though she was my aide, moving between the lab and the classroom, purposefully helping her classmates and solving problems.	This week had its ups and downs for Joann. For the first time, her teammates started showing frustration with her trying to control everything. I intervened; we had a short team meeting and everything was amicably resolved.	Overall, this was an okay week for Joann. I did need to calm her down a bit on Wednesday as the party and unstructured format was a little too much stimulation for her. I don't think she liked the prep work for the writing assessment, but she stayed on task and was respectful.	Joann was cooperative during the writing assessment, although I don't know how well she did yet. She was absent for the movie and was cooperative on the field trip, but that may have been because her mom was one of the chaperons.

127

Figure 8.18   Student Self-Assessments of Effort by Achievement Level

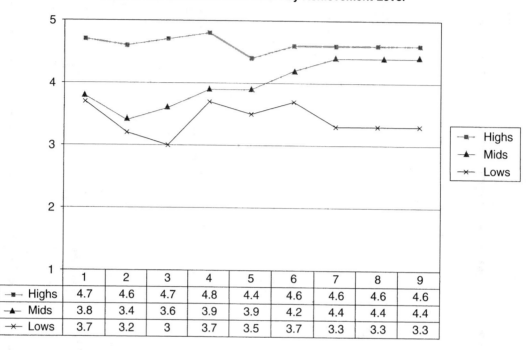

Student Self-Assessment of Effort by Achievement Level

	1	2	3	4	5	6	7	8	9
Highs	4.7	4.6	4.7	4.8	4.4	4.6	4.6	4.6	4.6
Mids	3.8	3.4	3.6	3.9	3.9	4.2	4.4	4.4	4.4
Lows	3.7	3.2	3	3.7	3.5	3.7	3.3	3.3	3.3

Figure 8.19   Student Self-Assessments of Effort by Gender

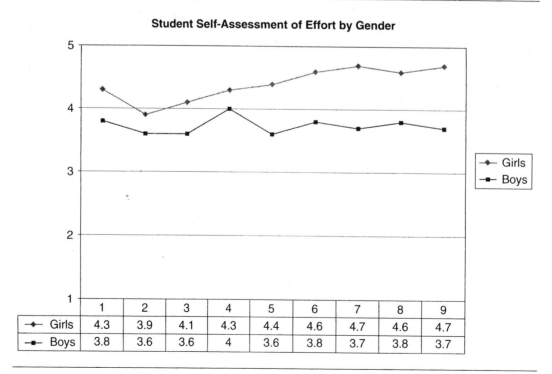

Student Self-Assessment of Effort by Gender

	1	2	3	4	5	6	7	8	9
Girls	4.3	3.9	4.1	4.3	4.4	4.6	4.7	4.6	4.7
Boys	3.8	3.6	3.6	4	3.6	3.8	3.7	3.8	3.7

NOTE: These scores are based on a five-point rubric and are entered by the teacher at the end of each week for each student. This type of assessment could just as easily be conducted and entered by the teacher on a daily basis while walking about the classroom.

DRAWING TENTATIVE ASSERTIONS ■

At this point, review the statements (findings) you've written and reflect on how these findings might be explained. Your reflections at this stage are what researchers call *tentative assertions,* and they combine two things:

- Empirical data (every one of your findings, the bulleted narrative statements)
- Your intuition regarding the influence of actions on performance

You shouldn't be uncomfortable with the use of intuition in this context, even if you are a novice action researcher. After all, while you may be new to action research, you aren't new to the world of the classroom. You've been an active participant in the actions that you've been studying and, in all probability, this is not your first year of teaching; consequently, you are an experienced and sensitive observer of the teaching and learning process. If you have a sense of why one thing impacted another and why it did so in the particular way it did, it certainly warrants being noted as an educated hypothesis.

Mr. Seeker might tentatively assert the following concerning his study of improving effort and engagement in writing:

> The drop in average performance appeared to be a reflection of a decline in student motivation likely influenced by a shift of classroom focus from the writing process to reviewing for the state exam. This observed drop in performance was most pronounced with the boys and with students with a history of moderate and low performance. I suspect the reason why there wasn't a comparable decline in the performance of the high achievers was that these kids are so habitually committed to getting good grades that it didn't matter to them if the work was particularly motivating or interesting. The girls in this class are a very cooperative and responsible group, and this may explain why they continued to work hard even though their feedback made it clear they found the work to be less stimulating. My guess is that the slight improvement in the girls' performance (even though they didn't like it) was due to the review work being significantly less challenging than what we had been doing previously.

As has been mentioned several times in this text, we can't prove nor should we contend to have proven causal relationships. This simply cannot be done in action research or in any other form of social science. Instead, our goal as practitioner researchers is to identify relationships and correlations that appear so strong and occur so consistently that it only makes sense to adjust our future actions in a way that is consistent with those findings.

The way we build confidence in the importance of a relationship is by establishing as best we can that the relationship or correlation was more than mere coincidence. In the rest of our lives we do this all the time, and we do it intuitively. In fact, we do it the same way that scientists do: through repeated trials and attempts to accomplish the same thing in the same manner and seeing if we can replicate the results. This is nothing new to the classroom teacher; we do this routinely with our teaching. When something appears to have worked, we try it again. If it works the second time and with another group, it builds our confidence, and we probably stick with it. The more this pattern repeats itself, the more confident we become regarding the efficacy of the approach.

That having been said, often our action research is a first-time trial. Therefore, before we can comfortably and confidently move ahead with our answers to

Question 3, we ought to consider how we might add more credibility and validity to our "tentative assertions."

■ USING MEMBER CHECKING TO ADD CREDIBILITY TO THE TENTATIVE ASSERTIONS

Member checking is a strategy that qualitative researchers often use to add support for and provide insight into their tentative assertions. As the name implies, this is accomplished by checking with the members of the group whose behavior or performance was documented. We do this by following two sequential steps:

Step 1: The researcher shares the *findings* with the members of the group whose work was chronicled. By findings, we mean the pertinent facts, the bulleted narrative statements, not the interpretations of those facts. For example, referring to the changes in performance Mr. Seeker observed as coincidental with time spent reviewing for the state test, the findings that he would share with his students might be as follows:

1. Average class performance declined during the period of preparation for the state exam.

2. Average performance of the boys declined sharply during the period of preparation for the state exam.

3. The average performance of the average- and low-performing students declined during the period of preparation for the state exam.

4. There was no significant change in performance of the high-achieving students during the period of preparation for the state exam.

5. There was a slight improvement in performance of the girls during the period of preparation for the state exam.

6. All students reported that the class work was less fun and less stimulating during the time we were preparing for the state exam.

Step 2: This step can be done in either of two ways. The first is to follow your report of findings by posing an open-ended question to the members (in this case, the students in the class): *How would you interpret these findings?*

Another approach is to go ahead and share your interpretation of the facts, your statement of tentative assertions, and then ask the membership, *Do you think my interpretation is correct? And if not, how would you explain these findings?*

When the perceptions of an educated observer and the members of the group whose performance was documented are in agreement, significant credibility is added to the tentative assertions.

Occasionally when we conduct member checking, we find that the members disagree with us. This could mean that our tentative assertions were, in fact, incorrect. Alternatively, it might mean there is another way to explain the same findings. Sometimes, after considering the additional data that surface through member checking, action researchers will change their tentative conclusions. Other times, they will still feel justified in their original positions. On still other occasions, the interpretations that surface though member checking are used to modify and add texture to the conclusions drawn by the researcher. Regardless of the outcome, member checking always provides valuable insights to our understanding of the impact of action on performance.

The preceding section focused on analyzing data collected to answer the three generic ACR action research questions. Those strategies are also applicable for many other action research questions. However, if the trend analysis processes that we have looked at so far do not appear appropriate for analyzing the data you have collected, then the tools that follow will hopefully help you in your search for the story embedded in your data. But even if the trend analysis strategies presented thus far appeared suited for your action research questions, I still suggest that you read through the following section and consider these additional approaches prior to concluding your analysis of data, as these tools might help you develop an even deeper understanding of the story in your data.

ADDITIONAL TOOLS FOR DATA ANALYSIS ■

As we continue our look at data analysis, it would be helpful to use a metaphor from the world of athletics. A key element of the preparation for competition in most sports is *scouting,* a systematic process of observing the competition, reviewing statistical data on their performances, and developing a list of their tendencies. Tendencies are for athletes what correlations are for statisticians—a set of findings drawn from data on past action. A tendency reports a pattern as follows:

When x is the *context* and y is the *action,* then z tends to be the *response.*

Having a good set of tendencies is important for an athlete or coach preparing for competition because it enables him or her to predict the consequences of an action with a certain degree of confidence. For example, let's assume I am a baseball pitcher. It is the ninth inning, there are two outs, and the batter has two strikes. I must decide where to throw my next pitch. Now, let's say I know that this batter has a tendency to swing at an inside fastball when in this situation, perhaps 90% of the time. If I want him to swing at my next pitch, based on my knowledge of this tendency, I will throw an inside fastball. In this example, *the context* is the behavior of this particular batter in ninth-inning pressure situations. *The action* is throwing an inside fastball, and *the response* is a swing (90% of the time).

Tendencies allow us to plan future action for a given context based on a pattern of past responses to those same actions in that same context. That is precisely what most of us hope to gain from the analysis of our action research data. So as you go through the process of analyzing your data, what you are trying to accomplish is the generation of a reliable list of tendencies. This necessitates sorting your data into two critical categories that will help with your final analysis:

- Things that will help you understand the context (especially as the context may have evolved over the period of the study)
- Things that will help you identify patterns of actions and the corresponding responses to those actions.

To illustrate the necessity of including all three things in our analyses—*context, action,* and *response*—I'll use an academic example. Figure 8.20 illustrates the average length of compositions produced by a group of students after their teacher introduced the word processor for writing. The reason this teacher started having her students use the computer for writing was because she theorized it would result in increased fluency.

Figure 8.20   Weekly Papers: Fluency, Weeks 1–3

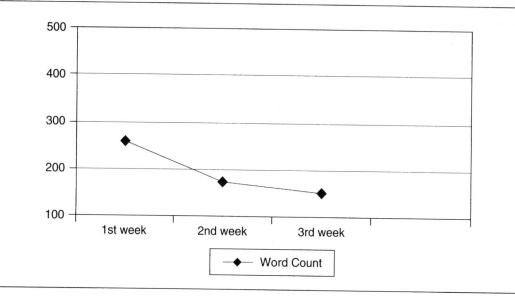

The story told by this graph shows that the average length of compositions actually decreased after the students began using word processing. *The action* in this case was the use of the word processor, and *the response* was fewer words per composition. This data could result in a finding that use of the word processor negatively influenced the development of fluency. The problem with that finding is not that it is based on erroneous data; the data is irrefutable. The problem is that it ignores some important nuances of *context*. To illustrate, we will now add two additional bits of data:

1. This was the first time these students had been exposed to this particular word-processing program.

2. This data reflects the papers written in the 3 weeks immediately following the introduction of the new software.

Figure 8.21 is a graph showing the average length of the weekly compositions, but now extended over the full course of the 9-week class.

Figure 8.21   Weekly Papers: Fluency, Weeks 1–9

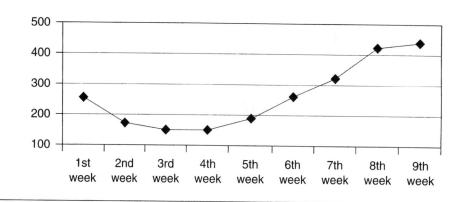

With the addition of these two bits of context, the data tell a very different story. The decrease in fluency that occurred in the first 3 weeks illustrates what Michael Fullan (2001) has called the *implementation dip,* a temporary phenomenon that often occurs when a new skill is being learned. Because of the awkwardness of integrating something new into old routines, performance often dips, but this is generally followed by improvement once the learner has become comfortable with the newly acquired skill.

LONGITUDINAL ANALYSIS USING BINS AND A MATRIX

We often find ourselves analyzing *qualitative* data that is difficult or impossible to convert into *quantitative* terms. For example, we may have collected data from interviews, from student or teacher journals, from the minutes of meetings, and so on. In those cases, it might be difficult to effectively use a graph to illustrate how our story is unfolding. Even so, the goal is the same: We are attempting to report on changes as well as degrees of change occurring over the time the actions took place. We still want to identify patterns and tendencies, but we will accomplish it in a different way.

The bins and matrix strategy, adapted from Miles and Huberman (1994), is a process of sorting and re-sorting action research data to identify and contrast tendencies and patterns as they exist in a particular context.

Creating Bins for Your Data

I see this process as analogous to the process of preparing the family's recyclables for curbside pickup. The waste management company supplied my family with four color-coded bins. The yellow one is where we are expected to place newsprint; the blue is for glass, the green for metal objects, and the red one is where we are expected to place our non-newsprint paper products. The task we face every time we carry a load to the garage is to look at each of the recyclables in our hands and determine which bin to put it in.

When using the bins and matrix process for sorting your action research data, you will be doing the same thing. Your first task is one that was done for my family by the waste management company. Using their experience and data, they determined what categories of recyclables to be collected. This resulted in the four bins: newsprint, glass, metal, and non-newsprint paper. Of course, each of their customers also consumed other products that could have been recycled: for example: wood products, engine oil, scrap metal, and plastic. Apparently, it was determined (after looking at data) that although many households possessed these other materials, they weren't doing so in large enough quantities to make it environmentally justifiable to send a fossil fuel-powered truck to collect these at the curbside.

Whenever I go to our garage with our recyclables, I sort my data into the bins that the company deemed relevant. One could look at my family's recycled items as data. In this particular case, the items accumulating in the bins in my garage are data on our family's consumption habits.

At this stage of the analysis process, the task at hand is to determine what bins or categories you deem to be most relevant. There are a number of things for you to consider when making this decision:

- The achievement targets your project was designed to impact
- The specific phenomena that your descriptive study was focused on
- The significant activities you engaged in or had your students engage in

In addition to those items, you should skim through the data you collected looking for issues, ideas, and actions that appear to have popped up over and over again. For example, if I were reading through a set of student reading journals, I might notice repeated comments regarding

- *Genres:* Fantasy, biography, and other nonfiction
- *Relevance:* Their reasons for being attracted to the work
- *Time issues:* Finding time to engage in recreational reading
- *Family attitudes* toward reading

Now it's time to go back and review your theory of action. Take another walk through your graphic reconstruction looking for the events or phenomena that you had, once upon a time (back when you developed your graphic), thought would be particularly relevant.

You are now ready to develop a list of potential bins.

For example, the elementary principal who was studying the development of a collegial culture in her school might have generated a list of bins like the following:

- Internal communication
- Problem solving
- Staff morale
- The school's Intranet discussion space
- Team planning
- Role of principal
- Student performance
- Faculty meetings

The next step is deliberately going through every individual piece of data you've collected or could get your hands on and placing that piece of data into the appropriate bin. When using this method, it is appropriate to use all the valid and reliable data that you have available, even if it came from on unanticipated source. The sorting process can be done using a variety of low-tech and high-tech methods. I will begin by discussing the low-tech process, since it is the most concrete, and then share a mechanism you may wish to consider that employs the word-processing or spreadsheet software that is likely already on your PC.

> As was the case with my family's recyclables, there may not be a bin for each item. However, if you did a good job of choosing bins, there should be a bin for the most important items. If you find you have lots of seemingly important data that can't be categorized, consider establishing more bins.

■ LOW-TECH STRATEGIES FOR BINS AND MATRIXES

Low-Tech Strategy 1: Making a Receptacle for the Data

I have done this in two ways. The first method is to purchase a set of small plastic bins, such as the ones shown in Figure 8.22, and labeling them with the categories of items to be collected in each.

A second approach is to take large rolls of chart paper, tape them to the wall, and create a column for each category.

Figure 8.22 Sorting Data Into Plastic Bins

When I'm using the plastic bins, I make sure I have a large quantity of index cards on hand. When using the chart paper, I make sure I have several colorful pads of Post-it notes available.

Placing the Data in the Bins

I now reread my data, looking for items that belong in one or more of my bins. I then write the piece of data verbatim on a Post-it or index card, indicate where it came from (e.g., from Joann Heathrow's journal, a parent's comment, a note from the principal), and note the date it was obtained or the date the event took place. The card is then placed into the appropriate plastic bin or attached in the proper column of the chart paper. Keep in mind that the same piece of data may be placed into multiple bins, if appropriate. Figure 8.23 shows an action research team placing their data into bins on chart paper.

This action research team was made up of master's degree students undertaking a descriptive study designed to identify the instructional practices most often used by local teachers with a reputation for obtaining high levels of student performance. They obtained so much data from six class observations that they needed an entire wall to effectively sort their data.

Other Low-Tech Strategies: Cutting and Pasting and Using Highlighters

One very efficient strategy when using data collected from surveys or written work (provided they won't have to be returned) is to make use of only one side of each sheet (unfortunately, this is not an environmentally friendly strategy, but it does make analysis easier). Whenever a piece of data surfaces that belongs in a bin, simply cut it out (always being sure to indicate where it came from and when it was obtained), and then physically place it into or paste it onto the appropriate bin. Another approach makes use of highlighting pens. When I do this, I assign a color to each bin. If I have a very large number of bins, I will assign a symbol as well as a color.

Figure 8.23   Placing Data Into Bins

■ HIGH-TECH STRATEGIES FOR BINS AND MATRIXES

High-Tech Strategy: Using the Sort Command

It can be very time-consuming to retype data into a computer's word-processing program or onto a spreadsheet. For this reason, using this next approach will not make sense unless you are a proficient typist or have clerical support available. However, should you have your data already in a word processing format or can place it onto a spreadsheet, then the sorting function contained in all word-processing and spreadsheet programs will enable you to sort your data into bins very quickly. Follow these steps:

Assign a number to each category. For example, with Dr. Hernandez's study of collegiality, these might be the assigned numbers:

1. Internal communication

2. Problem solving

3. Staff morale

4. Intranet discussion space

5. Team planning

6. Role of principal

7. Student performance

8. Faculty meetings

Then, when typing or retrieving pertinent text, type in the appropriate number at the beginning of the passage, and hit the return key both before and after each "coded" item, transforming it into a separate paragraph. For example, assume I found a quote from a teacher survey that belonged in the bin for staff morale. I would have that item read as follows:

> 3. Honestly, I hated going to meetings at this school; I even dreaded reading the staff bulletin. Nothing that we ever did seemed relevant to me. But now I look forward to working together; the meetings have truly helped me enjoy my job.

Then by simply using the "sort" command (most word processing and spreadsheet programs have a sort function), all items belonging in a particular bin are instantly put together. Another nice aspect of using the computer to sort the data is that you can easily re-sort and subsort the data inside individual bins—a very helpful tool for disaggregation purposes. This is accomplished by thinking through in advance all the subcategories you might ever want to sort by and reflecting on the order in which you would want to have them sorted. For example, the order I might want to sort data could be

First, by bin

Second, by whether the item is positive or negative

Third, by the grade level where it originated

Then a number is assigned to each of the subcategories (e.g., positive = 1, negative = 2; 1 = first grade, 2 = second grade). Then, in the prearranged order of sorting, I input the code numbers. Using the foregoing codes as an illustration, if the quoted passage had come from a second-grade teacher, the item would be prefaced by the numbers 3.1.2, meaning it is a comment on staff morale (3), it is a positive comment (1), and it is from a second-grade teacher (2).

There is virtually no limit to how many subcategories you can create. And whatever process you ultimately decide to use for sorting your data, be sure to create a coding key for easy referencing later on. Take a look at the following illustration of a sample key that Dr. Hernandez might have established to guide and explain the sorting of data into bins.

Level 1	Level 2	Level 3	Level 4
Bin	Tone	Grade Level	Date Obtained
1 = Internal communication	1 = Positive	1 = First	1 = September
2 = Problem solving	2 = Negative	2 = Second	2 = October
3 = Staff morale		3 = Third	3 = November
		4 = Fourth	4 = December
			5 = January

Create Factoids From the Information in the Bins

After you have sorted all the data you deemed relevant, it is time to go through the items in each bin, generating brief bulleted statements of fact that can be supported by the data contained in that bin. Then write each factoid on a separate index card. What qualifies something as a factoid is your professional judgment regarding its significance. I find that I generally create two kinds:

1. *Statistical:* I report both the quantity and percentage of items that report on the same thing (for example, 13 comments, from 20% of the teachers, were complimentary of the principal's leadership).

2. *Illustrative:* If a comment or a vignette helps bring a statistic to life, I write it verbatim on a separate card (for example, typical of the positive comments on principal leadership was this comment from a sixth-grade teacher: *"It was clear that Elena [the principal] kept the district from making demands on the faculty that would draw us away from the school goals. I really appreciate that. It showed me that she really was supportive of our priorities."*)

The factoids the waste management company might create, after reviewing the data in my family's recycling bins, might read like these:

- In an average week, this family disposes of
  - 47 mail order catalogues
  - 64 pop cans, 40% of which are sugar free
  - 15 newspapers (none of which appear to have been read)
  - No more than one tin can

- Most weeks, the man of the household comes running out of the house in his bathrobe with additional items to be added at the last minute.

The data in a bin on staff morale might produce factoids like the following:

- 80% (16) of the comments on the April evaluation were positive.
- 55% (11) of the comments in the September evaluation were positive.
- A typical comment from a fifth-grade teacher (April evaluation): "Honestly, I used to hate going to meetings at this school. I even dreaded reading the staff bulletin. Nothing that we ever did seemed relevant to me. But now I look forward to working together; it has truly helped me to enjoy my job."
- 80% (8) of comments made by intermediate teachers in the September evaluation were negative in nature.
- 20% (2) of the comments by the intermediate teachers in the April evaluation were negative in nature.
- 12 comments on the April evaluation referred to positive actions by the principal.
- There were no negative comments (regarding morale) that referenced the principal.

Sift the Data Using a Matrix

Keep in mind that our main purpose when engaged in data analysis is to identify and communicate an evolving story. Every story has a context and occurs over time. To find the story, we need to see the patterns of meaningful action and identify the tendencies of the responses that followed those actions. Occasionally, this happens by the simple sorting of data into bins. However, more often, further sorting of the data is needed to enable the full story to emerge. One good way to do this is to make use of two-dimensional matrixes. Figure 8.24 shows the general structure of a matrix set up for analyzing the data from Dr. Hernandez's study of faculty collegiality.

Each bin becomes a column in the matrix, while the rows could be assigned a variety of different values. Since I am often interested in understanding how a story unfolded, I usually begin by assigning time frames to the rows (fall, winter, spring

Figure 8.24 Two-Dimensional Matrix for Data Analysis

	Communication	Problem Solving	Staff Morale	Intranet	Team Planning	Principal's Actions	Student Data	Faculty Meetings

Copyright © 2005 Corwin Press. All rights reserved. Reprinted from *The Action Research Handbook: A Four-Step Process for Educators and School Teams*, by Richard Sagor. Thousand Oaks, CA: Corwin Press, www.corwinpress.com. Reproduction authorized only for the local school site that has purchased this book.

or monthly, weekly, etc.). Then the factoids that I generated are placed into the appropriate cells of the matrix.

Summarize and Draw Tentative Conclusions

Once my time-frame matrix has been completed, I review the rows and columns and ask myself whether this data answers my research questions. If it does, then I summarize the data in the form of tentative assertions.

Often, the answers to all your questions will not be apparent from one matrix, and you will need to repeat the process using different categories for the rows. Keep in mind, your purpose is always the same: identifying meaningful patterns and tendencies. The time frame matrix will highlight the relationship between changes in performance and time. Likewise, a gender matrix would highlight the relationship between gender and changes in performance. To properly answer your questions, you might want to examine other relationships; you will be able to do so relatively easily by simply changing the categories for the rows. Some of the categories that others have found helpful are

- Categories of participants
  - High achievers, middle achievers, low achievers
  - Gender
  - Ethnicity
  - English-language learners, English-proficient students
  - Primary teachers, intermediate teachers, middle school teachers, high school teachers

- Type of data
  - Interviews
  - Surveys
  - Portfolios
  - Teachers' journals

- Source of data
  - Students
  - Parents
  - School staff

Use Member Checking to Add Credibility to Your Findings

Once you have determined a set of tentative conclusions that you feel adequately respond to your research questions, it is time to test your perceptions against those of other participant observers of the same process. This is done by using the process of member checking that was discussed earlier in this chapter.

This concludes our discussion regarding the analysis of action research data. Analysis ends with us acknowledging what we've learned through our actions. In the next chapter, our focus shifts to action planning where we deal with the bottom-line question for all action researchers,

Now that we know this, what are we going to do about it?

9

Turning Findings
Into Action Plans

In Chapter 8, we began working through the final stage of the action research process—Stage 4: Reflecting on the Data and Planning Informed Action. This stage has three parts: analyzing, action planning, and reporting. In the last chapter, we covered data analysis where our purpose was finding the story embedded in our action research data. The analysis process concluded with the generation of a list of findings and tentative conclusions backed up with data.

Whether your action research was descriptive or quasi-experimental, the analysis process should have resulted in greater clarity on what had actually occurred in the pursuit of your achievement targets. The insights provided through analysis were probably meaningful for you for a number of reasons.

The greatest value of what we learn from our action research lies in the power of the new knowledge and the insights we gained for informing our future actions and consequently providing benefits for our students. This value is realized when we make use of our findings and conclusions to make adjustments to our mode of practice and generate new operative theories of action.

MODIFYING YOUR THEORY OF ACTION ■

If we are to be reflective practitioners, the thing we must always do before commencing action is to reflect deeply on what we know about the challenges that lie ahead and use that thinking to design a thoughtful theory of action to guide our work. The processes we employed to accomplish this involved two visual aids, the priority pie and the graphic reconstruction. Now that we have concluded our action and analyzed the data, it is time for us to return to these two documents and modify them based on what we now know.

A classic way to illustrate change over time is by contrasting *before* and *after* pictures. A graphic reconstruction is a type of *before* picture, a sketch of our best thinking *before* initiating action and prior to conducting our investigation. The *after* picture is a portrait of our best thinking after completing our study. In Chapter 5, I shared my revisionist history, asserting that Christopher Columbus was one of the earliest educational action researchers, and I suggested that a map by Henricus Martellus, circa 1489 (Figure 5.1), was the type of graphic reconstruction that likely guided Columbus on his first voyage—his "before" picture. For a comparison "after" picture, we could use Figure 9.1. This is a map drawn by John Speed in 1627, 138 years after Columbus's voyage.

The difference between these maps illustrates the increased understanding of planet earth by Western European geographers as they integrated the action research findings of Columbus, Magellan, Cabot, Cook, and others.

When we initially articulated our theories of action, we constructed a priority pie and produced a graphic reconstruction. At this point you would be wise to redo both of these visuals based on what you've learned through the analysis of the data you collected on your action (Chapter 8). However, this time I suggest that you prepare these documents in reverse order: draw your graphic first and then bake your pie.

Step 1: Taking Stock of What You Have Learned

Review your list of findings and the tentative assertions you drafted (see Chapter 8). Then take out the graphic reconstruction, the implementation roadmap you designed prior to implementation (Chapters 4 and 5). Now, one last time, take a slow and deliberate walk through your graphic reconstruction, asking a set of questions of every event or activity and relationship or cluster of relationships you encounter along the way.

For Every Activity or Event, Ask,

Based on what I've learned, do I now think that

1. There were other critical events or activities that should have occurred before engaging in this activity?
2. This activity is still necessary to achieve success with this target?
3. There are additional activities that ought to be added to improve performance on this target?

For Each Relationship or Cluster (Arrows, Linking Lines, and Groups of Events), Ask,

Based on what I've learned, do I now think that

1. This relationship is still important?
2. These activities or events influence each other in the manner illustrated?
3. There are other relationships that should be added to this theory?

Based on your answers to those questions, make all the additions, deletions, and alterations to your graphic reconstruction that you now deem necessary.

Once you have made the changes you feel are warranted, proof your new graphic reconstruction, as you did in Chapter 5. Once you are satisfied that your new graphic reconstruction illustrates a theory of action with real promise for producing universal success on your priority achievement targets, you have created your "after" picture.

Now place your before and after pictures side by side. Figure 9.2 contains Ms. Pioneer's before and after graphic reconstructions.

Figure 9.1   John Speed's 1627 Map

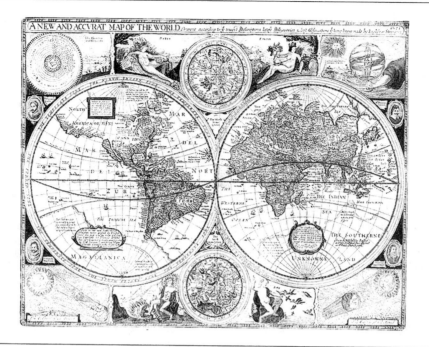

SOURCE: http://www.henry-davis.com/MAPS/Ren/Ren1/464.html

On close examination of Figure 9.2, one can see that Ms. Pioneer made two significant changes in her theory of action regarding the teaching of this unit based on her action research:

1.   Prior to conducting her research, she felt it was a good idea to randomly group and regroup her students for each project. But her data revealed a significant disparity between the functioning of the groups. It seemed that random assignments didn't always result in groups with a productive chemistry. Based on this data, she now believes that student groups would function better if she strategically assigned students based on her analysis of their strengths and needs.

2.   In her earlier theory, she had left the development of work plans completely to the members of each group, with no teacher input. She did this because she felt this would contribute to student ownership of the final projects. But her data told a different story. Several groups stumbled along and wasted valuable time when they could have been developing their plans, causing some students to become frustrated and force their ideas on other group members, which undermined group cohesiveness. Furthermore, two of the groups' work plans were so inadequate that it made creating a quality product very difficult. As a result of these findings, she now plans to have the groups negotiate their work plans directly with her, prior to executing them.

Step 2: Reconsider the Time Issue

To begin this step, locate your original priority pie, which represents how you had thought your time and energy should be allocated to achieve universal success on your priority target. If you completed the Time Priority Tracking Table (Figure 8.4) and constructed a second pie that reflected the actual time usage, this is a good time

Figure 9.2   Before and After Graphic Reconstructions

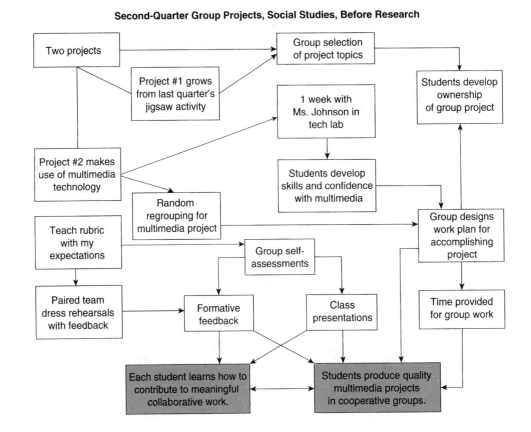

Second-Quarter Group Projects, Social Studies, Before Research

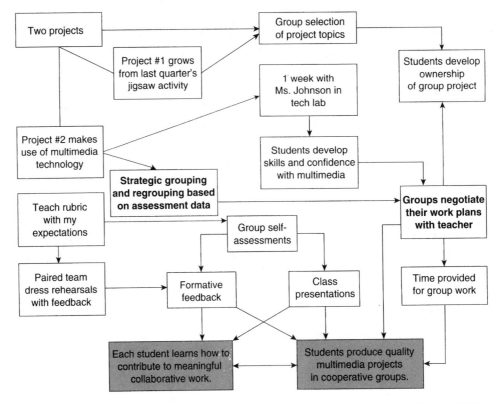

Second-Quarter Group Projects, Social Studies, After Research

to review them. Take a good look at the graphic reconstruction you just developed (your "after" picture), and conduct another intuitive regression analysis using Figure 9.3 (this form was used earlier in the text as Figure 4.1) and create a third pie graph. This one will illustrate how you now think your time *should* be allocated.

Figure 9.4 shows the before and after pies created by Ms. Pioneer. You can see that based on her research, she has generated an entirely new category of action (a brand new slice of pie): *coaching students on the development of work plans.* She appropriated the time for this new activity by reducing the time she had previously devoted to team building and group work.

Now place your original priority pie next to the one you just produced. A comparison of these two pie graphs should illustrate some of the insights gained through your research and help you better plan for the allocation of your finite time and energy next time around.

DATA-BASED DECISION MAKING ∎

The Use of Ed Specs

Frequently, when organizations such as schools begin planning for a major purchase or enter into a long-term contract, they start the decision-making process by developing a set of bid specifications. For school architecture and school facility development, those specifications are usually called *ed specs,* which later become the criteria used to evaluate competing proposals. Using a quality set of ed specs can go a long way toward ensuring that the decisions that are ultimately made are sound.

As you plan future action in your focus area, you have many programs and strategies to consider and consequently would be well served to have a sound set of criteria (ed specs) to help you make wise decisions. One very good place to find them is in the insights gained from the action research you just conducted and any research that was conducted in the recent past by you and your colleagues.

To understand precisely how this process works, it is instructive to review how it works in other educational arenas (e.g., school facility development and purchasing) and then adapt it for our purposes.

Ed Specs and School Facilities

Generally the process begins with a meeting of the people with the best knowledge of the current situation to take stock of the context and evaluate the operative theories of action. That information is then used to develop a list of specific things that are to be accomplished by the new facility or equipment.

A few years ago, I was working for a school district that was about to commence construction on a number of elementary schools. A staff committee had reviewed everything they knew about best practices for elementary education and theorized that in future decades, children would be spending nearly equal portions of their time at school engaged in individual, small-group, and large-group learning. Therefore, they wanted their new elementary schools to be designed to effectively accommodate all three types of learning activities.

There were also several givens (what we might call contextual issues) that needed to be taken into account. One was the state funding formula, which established the maximum square footage of the buildings and the amount of money available for construction. This meant that the designs produced by the district's architect would

Figure 9.3 Intuitive Regression Analysis

Using the following form, make a judgment regarding the relative importance of each of the factors you identified as critical to success on this achievement target. (Use a separate form for each target you are pursuing.)

Achievement Target: _____

List Each Factor Deemed Critical to Fostering Success With This Achievement Target	Importance of This Factor (%)
Total:	100%

Copyright © 2005 Corwin Press. All rights reserved. Reprinted from *The Action Research Handbook: A Four-Step Process for Educators and School Teams*, by Richard Sagor. Thousand Oaks, CA: Corwin Press, www.corwinpress.com. Reproduction authorized only for the local school site that has purchased this book.

have to fit within the state's cost and size restrictions. Nevertheless, it was important that the architect provide as many alternative designs as possible, each of which could accommodate the future needs of staff and students for consideration. Consequently, every design proposal was required to meet the demands of the future program as developed by the ed specs committee (equal opportunities for individual, small-group, and large-group instruction) as well as meeting the state regulations.

By only considering designs which addressed both categories of considerations, the district ensured that their new facilities would meet their needs. Before we translate this process to your action planning, it will be helpful to look at another nonclassroom application, one that is a little closer to the issues we are facing.

Ed Specs for Purchasing Computers

This second example of ed specs involves what may at first seem like a routine purchasing decision. In all likelihood you work in a school system that regularly purchases significant numbers of computers for student and teacher use. Since there are a number of manufacturers that produce and market computers for schools and there

Figure 9.4   Comparison of Priority Pies

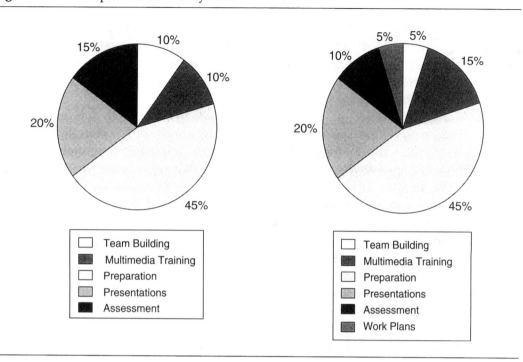

are several different operating systems to choose from, there are always many proposals to consider. As a great deal of money is at stake and since, for budgetary reasons, schools must live with the computers they buy for several years, it is important that wise choices be made. Therefore, prior to soliciting bids, most school systems create a set of purchasing criteria for use in evaluating the alternative proposals submitted by perspective vendors. Usually those criteria cover a multitude of factors:

Cost and Reliability

- The purchase price per PC
- The past defect record of these computers

Service

- Availability of onsite personnel for routine repairs
- Turnaround time for repairs that need to occur at the vendor's site

Versatility

- The ability of the computers to run the needed software
- Ease of use
- Availability of inservice and technical support
- Quality of the user manuals

Those making the final decision on which computers to purchase will insist that every bid address each one of these criteria and ultimately will choose the vender whose proposal scores best on the criteria. Inevitably, some proposals score better on certain elements than others. This is why it is crucial that each criterion be weighed based on importance.

Weighing Assessment Criteria

When you look at the above list above of criteria that could be considered when purchasing computers, you can easily see that they are not of equal importance. For instance, although having high-quality user manuals would be nice, even the best written documentation won't make up for computers that turn out to be unreliable, break down, and take forever to get fixed.

This is why when developing ed specs, one needs to take care to determine which factors are the *most critical*—so important that going ahead with a plan that does not satisfy this criteria is simply foolhardy. Other criteria, while not absolutely essential, will be deemed *highly desirable*. Last, there are criteria that are *valuable*, involving things we would like to have but which, like superlative user manuals, are not absolutely crucial to program success. When we are making data-based decisions, those distinctions need to be made *prior* to evaluating competing proposals.

Now we return to concerns more central to the life of the classroom teacher, the type of program planning decisions that you make on a regular basis and which ultimately determine the success of the actions you take in the classroom. We can see how the same principles of data-based decision making can be applied to instructional planning.

■ TURNING YOUR FINDINGS INTO ED SPECS

The list of findings you generated in Chapter 8 can now become your first draft of ed specs for assessing the proposals for new programs or the design of novel innovations for use in your school or classroom. The form shown in Figure 9.5 was designed to help you convert your action research findings into ed specs.

In the left-hand column, write all of the bulleted findings that emerged from your data. Then convert these into ed specs; this is the middle column on the worksheet. Once you have listed all the findings as ed specs, it is time to ask,

How important is this particular ed spec to the decisions I must make on my future actions?

Based on your answer, rate each finding using the following scale:

5 *Essential factor* (Programs that do not address this ed spec aren't appropriate for use here.)

3 *Important factor* (Programs or actions that address this ed spec should be of significant help in improving performance with my priority achievement target.)

1 *Worthy factor* (Programs or actions that address this ed spec are better suited for use than those that do not.)

When using action research findings for ed specs, you needn't limit yourself to the findings from your most recent study. Findings from studies conducted by other teachers or other relevant data on the needs of your context can also be used.

Figure 9.5 Turning Research Findings Into Ed Specs

Step 1: List all the pertinent findings from your and other research in this focus area.

Step 2: Write the essence of the finding in the form of an educational specification.

Step 3: Determine the weight to be assigned to this ed spec, with 5 indicating the highest effectiveness:

Pertinent Action Research Finding	*Finding Rewritten as an Ed Spec*	*Weighting: 5, 3, or 1*
Example: Time for writing was limited due to preparation for the state assessment.	The need for additional time for use with the writing process.	5—Essential factor

Copyright © 2005 Corwin Press. All rights reserved. Reprinted from *The Action Research Handbook: A Four-Step Process for Educators and School Teams,* by Richard Sagor. Thousand Oaks, CA: Corwin Press, www.corwinpress.com. Reproduction authorized only for the local school site that has purchased this book.

■ SOLICIT AND BRAINSTORM ACTION ALTERNATIVES

At this point, it is time to return to the graphic reconstruction you completed at the end of the analysis process. This is the graphic that illustrated your *revised* theory of action. Take a look at the changes you made to your original theory and ask yourself (or your teammates) what strategies you are aware of that have been used elsewhere in an attempt to achieve success with the achievement targets. To illustrate how this might be done, let's return once again to the case of Ms. Pioneer.

In her revised theory of action (Figure 9.2), she noted two significant changes in the way she thought this particular unit should be implemented next year:

1. Strategically assign students to cooperative groups.

2. Have the groups negotiate their work plans with the teacher.

For dealing with the issue of strategic grouping, she quickly came up with a list of possible approaches:

1. My students could submit a "most wanted to work with" list and I could use this data to make group assignments.

2. I could rank the students by past performance and select groups to maximize heterogeneity.

3. I could rank the students by past performance and assign groups to maximize homogeneity.

4. I could assign the students to single-gender groups.

5. I could use random assignments modified by my personal perceptions of student compatibility.

The different strategies on her list are called action alternatives. Each one is an approach that, on the surface, appears to have promise for fulfilling Ms. Pioneer's needs. What she now needs to do is to choose which one of these action alternatives will likely work best for her students and with her program.

> If the list you have generated seems adequate, it is okay to proceed with that list. However, if you sense that you are unable to find strategies that hold promise to solve your problem, it is a good idea to conduct another literature review (see Chapter 3 if needed).

■ ASSESSING THE ACTION ALTERNATIVES

Having collected a comprehensive set of action alternatives, it is time to evaluate each one using the weighted ed specs you developed from the relevant findings. One way of doing this is by constructing a chart for each action alternative like the one shown in Figure 9.6. I usually do these using pieces of 3' × 5' chart paper.

Now you need to review the elements of each action alternative through the lens of your ed specs (Figure 9.5). Stand in front of each action alternative poster with your ed specs in hand and ask the following question regarding each one of your ed specs:

Figure 9.6 Sample Action Alternative Poster

Action Alternative: _____

Ed Specs in Support of AA	Points
_____	_____
_____	_____
_____	_____
_____	_____
_____	_____
_____	_____
_____	_____
Total Points Supporting:	_____

Ed Specs in Opposition of AA	Points
_____	_____
_____	_____
_____	_____
_____	_____
_____	_____
_____	_____
_____	_____
Total Points Opposing:	_____

Copyright © 2005 Corwin Press. All rights reserved. Reprinted from *The Action Research Handbook: A Four-Step Process for Educators and School Teams,* by Richard Sagor. Thousand Oaks, CA: Corwin Press, www.corwinpress.com. Reproduction authorized only for the local school site that has purchased this book.

Is the implementation of this action alternative likely to have a positive influence, negative influence, or no influence on this criterion?

Whenever your answer is *positive*, that ed spec and its weighted score should be placed on the top portion of the chart. If the answer is *negative*, then that ed spec and its number should be placed on the lower portion of the chart. If the answer to your question is *no influence*, then nothing is written on the chart.

Repeat this process with each of the action alternatives. Once each action alternative has been assessed using your set of ed specs, total the positive points (top portion of the chart) and subtract any negative points that have been assigned (the lower portion) to produce a score for that action alternative. Then list the action alternatives in rank order based on the point totals.

At this point, your decision-making process will differ from the bid procedure used by school business offices. Frequently, state or provincial laws require the awarding of contracts to the lowest bidder. This is a reasonable requirement that ensures fiscal accountability. However, as professionals who are using action research findings to improve their teaching and their students' learning, it makes no sense to be bound to a strategy simply because that strategy achieved a marginally higher score than a competing one.

When using this data-based decision-making process, you will generally find that your action alternatives fall neatly into three groups:

Group 1: Weak Proposals. Some action alternatives may, in fact, have obtained a negative score. This means that this particular approach would likely make things worse than the current situation.

Group 2: Adequate Proposals. A second group of alternatives will have received positive scores but a significant number of negative ones as well. Consequently, the total score is rather low. It probably is not worth the effort to alter your current approach, and go through all the work and possible expense of implementing a new program which, at best, will turn out to be only marginally superior to the approach you've been using.

Group 3: Strong Proposals. There will be action alternatives that received many positive scores from your ed specs and attracted very few, if any, negative ones. These are proposals that appear to hold real potential for making a difference in your efforts to produce universal success on your priority achievement targets.

Making a Final Decision on Action

It is now time to consider the applicability of each of the action alternatives in Group 3, the strong proposals. This is another point in the process where it is appropriate to use intuition. For each alternative, ask yourself these three questions:

- How well do these strategies fit my or our teaching style?
- How might the students in our school respond to this program or approach?
- What, if any, additional problems or expenses would this program entail?

If the project you are working on is a collaborative effort, it is well worth taking some meeting time to discuss these issues and employ a group decision-making process to decide on the particular action alternative that you all think fits best. In my experience, this is rarely a contentious decision. I might hold a preference for one of the high-scoring alternatives, while some of my teammates might be more attracted to another, but it is unlikely that I would have a strong objection to going along with their choice, since every proposal receiving final consideration was one that fit with our findings.

COMPLETING THE CYCLE: ■
REVISED THEORY OF ACTION 2

Unless you discovered the magic elixir that succeeded in getting every single student or every participant in your project to achieve excellent performance on your target, your work as a reflective practitioner and action researcher can't be considered complete.

What you have accomplished, however, is having completed one full lap around the action research cycle. (Reporting, which will be discussed in the next chapter, does not necessarily need to occur prior to beginning another cycle of action research.)

Figure 9.7 illustrates the relationship between the steps of repeated cycles of action research when done on the same targets by the same researchers. You are now nearly ready to restart the process. However, this time you will begin your work at Stage 3, with the establishment of a new set of research questions (see Chapter 6).

As you may recall, the process of developing meaningful action research questions required having a clear and unambiguous theory of action that you were committed to implementing. Therefore, the only thing left for you to do before commencing your second round of research is to do a final review of your revised theory.

Figure 9.7 Action Research Cycle

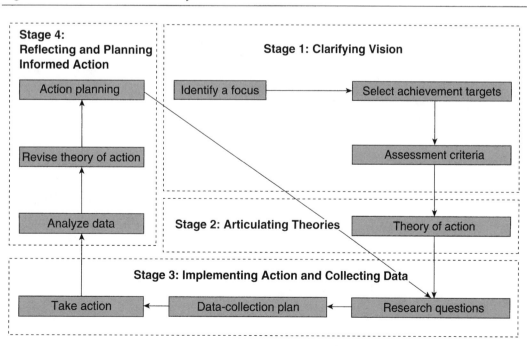

It is now time to examine the revised theory of action you developed earlier in this chapter and ask if it requires any further modification in light of the action alternatives you have just adopted, considered, or rejected for your program. If it does, you should insert those changes and alter your priority pie indicating any revisions in the proposed allocation of time and energy.

Once you are satisfied that you have a revised theory of action that captures your best current thinking, that is consistent with the findings of your research, and incorporates any action alternatives you are adding, you are ready to select a new set of research questions and rejoin the action phase of the process.

Hopefully, you aren't in too great a rush because in the next chapter we will discuss the very important topic of reporting and sharing your action research findings. Many action researchers, myself among them, have found that whenever our findings are presented to colleagues, a great deal is learned from their reactions and comments. Consequently, I usually like to share my findings with my peers and solicit their ideas before I jump into my next round of action.

10

Reporting and Sharing Action Research

There is nothing in the world of scholarship and science less controversial than the need for faithful and accurate reporting of results. From our earliest experiences studying science in school, to our professional endeavors, and even in our lives as consumers, we have all learned how important it is to be able to access accurate summaries of the experience of others to inform our own future actions and decisions.

In science class we learned that it isn't enough to conduct an experiment correctly; the results of that experiment must also be presented competently in a lab report. These are reasonable expectations for the science student because they parallel the real world of scientific practice. Reporting is so crucial to advancements in science that the scientific community has institutionalized processes for the sharing of findings that are rigorously followed throughout the world.

Presentations of findings are made at professional meetings and studies are reported in widely circulated journals. Papers are only accepted for publication or presentation after careful peer reviews for comprehensiveness, clarity, and accuracy. After initial review, research reports are publicly presented to knowledgeable and skeptical audiences who are expected to examine the findings as much to identify fatal flaws as to validate the accuracy of the findings. Scholarly debates are publicly reported in conference proceedings as well as in the pages of refereed journals and throughout the halls of academe.

As much as these processes are an esteemed part of the culture of the world of science, and as much as citizens have come to depend on the results of scientific sharing for the development of the products and services we consume, being an active participant in this scholarly presentation of research while working as a full-time teacher probably appears daunting at best.

However, if we overlook the crucial importance of the reporting process and choose not to engage in it, we do so at our own and at our sacred profession's peril. When we don't share what we've learned through our experience, we are forcing every other teacher and every other faculty to have to reinvent the wheel all by themselves. Furthermore, as sound as our analysis may have been, when we have additional eyes and ears considering and debating our findings, it inevitably leads to deeper and sharper understanding. All of our students suffer when their teachers aren't in possession of the very best information when making instructional decisions. Finally, when educators don't share what they're learning, it perpetuates teacher isolation and reinforces the myth that this amazingly complex work is actually rather simple and can be mastered by professionals working alone in their own cubicles.

The good news is that while self-interest—as well as our professional interests—requires the reporting of our action research, the process for sharing need not be onerous. There are as many ways and as many formats for reporting and sharing teacher research as there are teacher researchers. In this chapter, we take a look at a few reporting processes and formats, ranging from the simple to the complex, and discuss the circumstances that call for using different approaches. But first, we examine a set of common issues that should be considered whenever planning a report on action research.

■ COMMON ISSUES

Common Issue 1: Consider the Audience

As stated at the outset of this book, the primary reason for any of us to engage in action research is to help *us* learn from *our* practice to inform *our* future actions. Defined this way, every action research study already had an audience before it ever began, even if a small one: the actor him or herself. But even when working in a remote and isolated location, this is likely not the only potential audience for our work. Even if we are working in a one-room schoolhouse, our students, their parents, and the community will have a keen interest in the results of our inquiries. And if there is at least one other teacher in our school, there will be someone who is trying to teach a similar curriculum to similar students. It is a fair guess that our immediate colleagues will have at least a passing interest in hearing about the story told through our data. Last, since we are all part of the larger community of educators who are collectively engaged in a search for best practices, we can be sure that there are other teachers in other places who are grappling with the same issues and consequently will find our insights to be of particular interest.

One way to conceptualize the different potential audiences for our action research is to look at them as nested circles as illustrated in Figure 10.1.

The first consideration when preparing for sharing and reporting one's action research is determining who the principal audience (or audiences) will be for your report. Your answer will help you determine both the form and format that will work best for reporting on your work. Frequently, we are able to use our action research to kill multiple birds with one stone. For example, I might be studying the use of problem-based learning (PBL) in my science class. I am doing this primarily to improve my own skills. In addition, my school's annual school improvement plan is focused on making the science curriculum more relevant, and the implementation of PBL is an integral part of the plan. Coincidentally, I am enrolled in a master's program and am expected to complete an action research project to fulfill the research

Figure 10.1   Audiences for Action Research

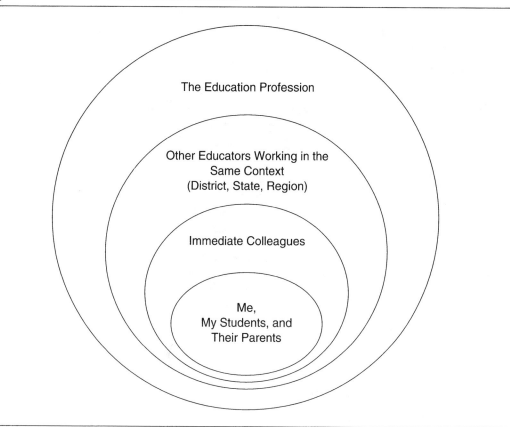

requirement for my degree. In a circumstance like this, the same piece of research—looking at the implementation of PBL with my fifth-period science class—could become the subject of three different research reports. However, each of these reports will need to satisfy different criteria.

Consider the levels displayed in Figure 10.1 and ask yourself which audience or audiences you will be aiming your report at:

- *Immediate audience.* Only those people with a direct interest in me, my students, and this class
- *Immediate colleagues.* The other teachers and educators with the responsibility for teaching this subject or these students: my grade level or department
- *Other educators in the same context.* Others in my district, region, state, or province
- *The larger educational community.* All K–12 educators and policy makers with an interest in educational settings similar to mine

Common Issue 2: Purpose—What Decisions Need to be Made?

All action research reports share one purpose: to help inform decisions on future action. In some cases there is only one decision to be made. However, there are occasions when a number of different decisions are influenced by the reports of research results. For example, if you were planning to submit your action research report as

Figure 10.2 Purposes of an Action Research Report

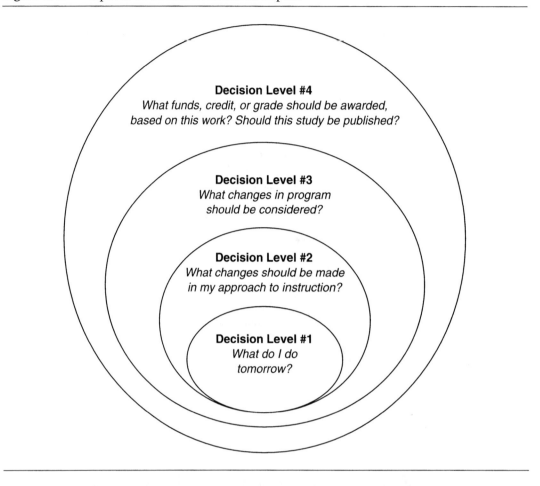

part of a master's program, in addition to providing you with information on instructional decision making as an instrument of accountability, your report will help the professor make a decision on your grade.

Many times, action research is used as part of the evaluation of an externally funded project. In such cases, the report is likely to influence decisions on whether this work should be continued and encouraged elsewhere. Often, educators find they are also interested in developing a scholarly publication record. These levels of decision making that can be influenced by action research reports can also be illustrated with a series of nested circles, as illustrated in Figure 10.2.

Common Issue 3: Degree of Detail

Every consumer of an action research report won't need or want the same degree of detail. The superintendent might have a keen interest in the efficacy of the new "standards-focused homework hotline" program and whether the three goals established by the school board for the program were being achieved:

- Enhanced parent-school communication
- Continuous improvement on the state standards
- More effective use of homework for learning

However, other aspects of the study may be more than is needed or wanted—for example, the specific nature of the homework assigned, how homework grades are determined, and patterns in homework assessments across individual teachers.

Here's another example: When presenting my research to my Language Arts Department colleagues, it might be enough to describe the context by saying, "This research was conducted with three sections of sophomore basic writing." But if I were presenting the same research study at a national conference for English teachers, I would need to provide significantly more detail on the nature of our school, its curriculum, and the type of students who are taking basic writing as sophomores. As you prepare for sharing, it is important to realize that you probably have already generated a great many documents and artifacts as you conducted your research:

- Your reflective writing
- Your priority pies
- Your graphic reconstructions
- Your data-collection matrix
- Any graphs or charts you made when analyzing data

All of these documents are items that you might choose to include in your report.

Occasionally, an action researcher will use the series of activities engaged in and the documents prepared as the *outline* for their report. By doing it this way, all that remains is to add a few minor transitions, explaining the rationale for your actions and the connections between them so that these decisions are clear to your audience.

The Report Planning Form (Figure 10.3) is a good place to begin the planning for your report. It should help you focus on the three common issues discussed earlier: audience, purpose, and detail.

FORMATS FOR REPORTING ■

I have seen compelling reports of action research projects in a wide range of formats. I've read articles written by teacher researchers in refereed journals, and I've seen action research shared informally in a teachers' lounge with a few colleagues sitting in a circle. I've watched teacher-produced videotapes that visually told the story of a research project, and I've seen research teams presenting their work on a stage at a large national convention. I've attending poster sessions held in school libraries with audience members moving from display table to display table, informally discussing the projects with the researchers.

At action research presentations, I've been given one-page handouts summarizing the findings, and at others I've received colorful, bound, 50-page written reports. Determining the appropriate format is a decision for you to make, based on your needs and those of your audience. While formats may differ, I have found that there is a flow and sequence that ensures that attendees will benefit from what was presented. This is a good time to once again remind ourselves that a completed action research report is basically a story. And just as there are infinite ways to write or tell a story, every story still contains a plot, starts from a beginning, and moves through a middle on the way to the end.

The report on your action research is the story of your trip through the four stages that framed this book:

Figure 10.3 Report Planning Form

Step 1: Determine who your audience will be.

Step 2: Reflect on the reason for their interest in your inquiry.

Step 3: Using the following table, review each of the steps you took in conducting your research, the activities you engaged in, and the documents you produced.

Step 4: Based on your determination of the audience's need (Step 1), decide which documents to share and which activities to describe.

Stage or Process	*Documents, Events*	*What Will You Share?*
Identify focus	Reflective writing, journaling, reflective interview	
Select achievement targets	List of priority achievement targets	
Literature review	Information gathered	
Develop assessment criteria	Rating scales for targets	
Develop theory of action	Priority pies and graphic reconstructions	
Research questions	List of questions	
Create data-collection plan	Triangulation matrix	
Action, collection of data	Raw data, vignettes	
Analysis of data	Revised graphic reconstruction and revised priority pie	
Action planning	Review of action alternatives	

Step 5: Using the following table, make a determination on both the detail called for and the presentation technique you will use for presenting the information you have decided to share.

Thing to Be Shared (from the right-hand column in the foregoing table)	*Detail Needed (e.g., summarized or with specifics)*	*Method for Sharing (handouts, displays, graphs, discussion, etc.)*

Copyright © 2005 Corwin Press. All rights reserved. Reprinted from *The Action Research Handbook: A Four-Step Process for Educators and School Teams,* by Richard Sagor. Thousand Oaks, CA: Corwin Press, www.corwinpress.com. Reproduction authorized only for the local school site that has purchased this book.

Stage 1: Clarifying Vision and Targets

Stage 2: Articulating Theory

Stage 3: Implementation and Collecting Data

Stage 4: Reflecting on Data and Planning Informed Action

As an audience member, I have found it particularly helpful when the person, video, or paper led me through the story of the researcher's inquiry in the same sequence as the four stages. Even when I'm unfamiliar with the focus area, I find it easy to follow a story that begins with this foundation:

- This is the context where I work (where my action takes place).
- This is what I was trying to accomplish (the vision I was pursuing and my targets).
- This is how I thought I could best accomplish it (my theory of action).

Once I have heard that background information, I am prepared to learn what happened next:

- This is what I did (the implementation of my theory of action).
- This is what data I collected along the way.

When I know what they were trying to accomplish and how they went about it, my appetite has been whetted to find out the ending:

- This is what I learned (my reflection on the data).
- This is what I intend to do about it (my action plan).

The Action Research Report Checklist (Figure 10.4) contains items that are often (although not always) addressed in an action research report. It is a good idea to go through this checklist prior to preparing your report. It should help alert you to items that you may want to consider including in your final product.

CREATING A BANK OF ABSTRACTS

Much has been written about the current knowledge explosion. In virtually every field, more and more information is being produced every single day. Finding efficient ways to access this information is becoming a necessity for people who want to stay current on their fields' knowledge base. The increased sophistication and ease of use of information technology, including publicly available Internet search engines, are making locating information much easier and will continue to do so. But there are other, more low-tech techniques that you and your colleagues might wish to consider.

One low-tech strategy for sharing, which many school systems have had success with, is the production of a readily accessible book of abstracts of locally conducted action research. For example, in the Madison (Wisconsin) Metropolitan School District, the books of action research abstracts now contain virtually hundreds of projects, spanning all the grades and every academic discipline. In many districts, each teacher is given a personal copy of the district's action research

Figure 10.4 Action Research Report Checklist

	Include? Yes or No
Characteristic 1: Explanation of Context, Problem, Issue	_____
Elements — Significance of issue for teachers and learners	_____
Unique or general factors impacting issue	_____
Potential for change/improvement	_____
Characteristic 2: Theoretical Perspective	_____
Elements — Summarize applicable literature	_____
Logic behind this particular approach	_____
Why not another approach?	_____
Characteristic 3: Research Design	_____
Elements — Why is it valid?	_____
Why is it reliable?	_____
How does it deal with extraneous or intervening variables?	_____
Characteristic 4: Analysis of Data	_____
Elements — The support and logic of the conclusions	_____
Alternative explanations of data	_____
Limitations explained	_____
Characteristic 5: Action Planning	_____
Elements — How is it supported by findings?	_____
Is its potential for improvement theoretically sound?	_____
Plans for further action research	_____
Outline of potential value for self and others	_____

Copyright © 2005 Corwin Press. All rights reserved. Reprinted from *The Action Research Handbook: A Four-Step Process for Educators and School Teams,* by Richard Sagor. Thousand Oaks, CA: Corwin Press, www.corwinpress.com. Reproduction authorized only for the local school site that has purchased this book.

catalogue (in hard copy or on a disk), or catalogues are made available in faculty rooms and through the district's media centers. These action research compilations are made user-friendly through cross-referencing by focus area, school subject, grade level, and program. Short abstracts provide enough information to enable a prospective user to get an idea of what has been investigated, without having to wade through a great many details. Then, if and when more information is desired, contact addresses, phone numbers, and e-mail addresses are provided. A particularly nice aspect of this approach is that writing a brief abstract doesn't take very long to accomplish.

Figure 10.5   Sample 300-Word Action Research Abstract

Topic	Example
Begin with a statement of the problem or the challenge being addressed by the research.	The faculty at Sagor Elementary has been impressed with the affective and academic benefits of cooperative learning. However, significant concern was expressed about the variance of productive engagement when cooperative activities are used. The purpose of this study was to help us understand the relationship of specific strategies with the level of engagement of our diverse learners. (57 words)
Then provide a brief description of the context of the research and the researchers.	Sagor Elementary School is a Title 1 school. Forty-two percent of Sagor students are English language learners. The study team consisted of two primary teachers and two intermediate teachers. (28 words)
Briefly describe the methodology of the study.	A teacher survey was used to determine the array of cooperative strategies being used at the school. A rating scale was developed to assess the degree of student engagement. During a 9-week period, four observations were made in each classroom where cooperative learning was used. The observers (10 teacher volunteers) used an engagement rating scale to assess the performance of nine students in each room (three low, three middle, three high achievers). (73 words)
Summarize the principal findings.	The data reflected a direct relationship between structure and both the amount of and variations observed in productive engagement. The four principal findings were as follows: 1. The more structured the activity, the higher the average level of engagement. 2. Average engagement dropped as the structures became more ambiguous. 3. In less-structured classrooms, the high achievers demonstrated slightly higher degrees of engagement. 4. In less-structured classrooms, middle and low achievers were significantly less engaged. (74 words)
State the conclusions, action plans, or additional research that resulted from this research.	After a presentation of the research, the faculty developed a continuum of cooperative strategies based on degree of structure. We are currently investigating strategic interventions designed to provide extra guidance and support for the middle- and low-achieving students with the use of the less-structured approaches. (47 words)

Figure 10.6 300-Word Action Research Abstract Worksheet

Topic	Response
Begin with a statement of the problem or the challenge being addressed by the research.	
Then provide a brief description of the context of the research and the researchers.	
Briefly describe the methodology of the study.	
Summarize the principal findings.	
State the conclusions, action plans, or additional research that resulted from this research.	

Copyright © 2005 Corwin Press. All rights reserved. Reprinted from *The Action Research Handbook: A Four-Step Process for Educators and School Teams,* by Richard Sagor. Thousand Oaks, CA: Corwin Press, www.corwinpress.com. Reproduction authorized only for the local school site that has purchased this book.

It is helpful to limit the length of an abstract. I have found the guideline of five paragraphs and 300 words works quite well. It can be accomplished by writing a straightforward paragraph in response to each of the following five prompts:

- State the problem or the challenge that was being addressed by this research.
- Provide a brief description of the setting of the research and the researchers (the context).
- Briefly describe the methodology used to collect data for this study.
- Summarize the principal findings.
- State the conclusions, action plans, or additional research that resulted from this research.

Figure 10.5 provides an example of an action research abstract written in response to the five prompts.

Now it's your turn. Try writing a 300-word abstract describing the study you just completed, using Figure 10.6.

CREATING A DISTRICT ARCHIVE ■

For several years, the Killeen (Texas) Independent School District has been building the professional development capacity of their district by providing 2-year grants to teachers who volunteer to document their work on innovative projects while working with a network of colleagues in the same focus area. At the end of the 2 years, participants prepare a written report for presentation to their colleagues, and the report then becomes part of a district-maintained knowledge base. The reports prepared by the Killeen teachers focus on the five characteristics found in Figure 10.4. Resource B contains a rubric that the Killeen teachers use as a guide when preparing their written reports.

It is strongly recommend that whenever one of the purposes of your action research report is to satisfy a requirement, mandate, or external expectation, you *request in advance the criteria by which it will be evaluated.* In most cases, the college, funder, or agency requiring the report will have established criteria that will help guide you through report preparation. If no criteria are available, you may want to consider using the rubric provided in Resource B as you develop your report.

11

Conclusion

The School as a Learning Organization

Dickens began *A Tale of Two Cities* with the line, "It was the best of times, it was the worst of times." The same thing could be said for the situation in which most of us K–12 educators currently find ourselves. I began this book discussing the context of the modern teacher. The expectations have never been higher, and it has never been more important that our graduates be well educated.

Becoming adults in our society without adequate language, reasoning, and learning skills places young people at risk of not being able to support themselves or their families. Students who leave school without a moral compass, an ability to appreciate beauty, and an adequate supply of self-confidence and self-esteem will find living a fulfilling life difficult at best. And modern democratic societies need citizens who are well grounded in the natural, social, and behavioral sciences.

Beyond the moral imperative of achieving universal success, increasingly punitive public policies are subjecting students, teachers, and the public schools to high-stakes sanctions if arbitrary benchmarks aren't met on a preordained schedule. None of this would be problematic if only we knew how to make universal success a reality. If it were possible that a fix for every teaching and learning problem could one day surface like a cure for a terrible disease, we could simply support the scientists working on these breakthroughs and eagerly await their great discoveries. But alas, the solution to education's challenges isn't likely to be found that easily.

As was discussed at the opening of this book, the acts of teaching and learning present problems that are among the most complex endeavors any professional ever has to deal with. And the front line workers in the education enterprise, the teachers and administrators working in schools, are the only people in a position to design adequate solutions to these challenges. Recruiting the best and brightest people to educate our children is arguably the most important issue facing modern society, and the future of public education rests solely on our ability to do so. Meanwhile, securing adequate funding for our schools and providing support for the people working in them is more tenuous than ever.

But there is also ample reason for optimism. Bright and capable people choose their careers based on an assessment of how rewarding the work will likely be. There are few things in the world of work more rewarding than working with colleagues trying to solve complex and important problems. It wasn't hard to persuade the rocket scientists at NASA and the medical researchers at the Salk Institute to work on their monumental breakthroughs. Likewise, nothing provides more joy for educators than seeing evidence of our students' growth and development. The best and most reinforcing thing about action research is that it creates a system for providing regular, credible data on student development while simultaneously enabling us to appreciate the role we have played in nurturing and facilitating that growth.

Teachers who integrate the four sequential stages of action research into their professional routines tend to be happy and satisfied professionals. Who wouldn't be happy when in possession of credible data on the success they were achieving while overcoming problems that have perplexed others for generations?

Anyone who has been involved in public education in recent years has been inundated with the surface trappings of modern organizational theory. It is a rare school or district that hasn't developed a vision and mission statement, backed up by a strategic plan. Those things are important, but inspiring words and elaborate plans are not what make organizations successful; rather, what makes for difference in performance are habits of behavior that are consistent with an organization's core values.

THE TWO KEYS: COHERENCE AND CONGRUENCE ■

Nobody needs a mission statement to know what the core value of schools should be in a democratic society. Surely, the business of public schools is maximizing the human potential of the next generation through growth, development, and mastery of a wide array of knowledge and skills. Accomplishing this requires organizational behavior that is consistent with the belief that everyone can learn, grow, and accomplish more than they had ever been able to do in the past. The two critical factors that determine whether an organization is staying true to its core values (behaving in accordance with its theory of action) are captured by the words *coherence* and *congruence*. Deliberate attention to the essence of the four stages of the action research process is one way for educators to ensure that the schools they work in manifest both of these elements.

Coherence

Schools are busy places. The typical teacher makes more decisions in 1 hour than most other people make in a day. Yet the question so often heard in the schoolhouse is, "Why are we doing this?" Principals ask this of the central office, teachers ask it of the curriculum, and students ask it of their teachers. When people are busy and are asked to do something but they are not sure why they are asked to do it and why they are required to do it a particular way, it is more than frustrating. It should be no surprise that a lack of clarity on goals and methods generally leads to increased alienation and a decrease in organizational effectiveness.

Fortunately, coherence is never lacking where teachers, schools, and students have integrated into their routines the first two stages of the action research process—*clarifying the vision and targets and articulating a rationale for pursuing a specific plan of action.* Publicly sharing the rationale behind what they are doing further builds coherence for those who are affected by their work.

Congruence

The educational process is about learning, and most every school's mission statement includes a recitation of the school's commitment to lifelong learning. But unfortunately, the behavior at many schools is far from consistent with that belief. The reality is that behavior is a more powerful teacher than words. When schools behave as though the authorities (teachers, administrators, professors, etc.) know all they need to know and have all the answers to the issues of practice, they are modeling a very different set of beliefs. The best way to convince our students of the value of lifelong learning is to let them see us cast in the role of learners. When students see the significant adults in their lives being curious, goal-driven people, trying to gain insight and knowledge from every experience they engage in, they will come to believe that we mean it when we say that learning is forever.

■ PUTTING THE PIECES TOGETHER

Jane Stickney, the former principal at Willamette Primary school in West Linn, Oregon, uses the phrase *the ethic of action research* to refer to the norms of collaboration and experimentation that prevailed at Willamette as she and her colleagues helped that school affect a remarkable turnaround in academic performance (Sagor, 1995). In schools such as Willamette, where the ethic of action research has been taken to heart, the system itself transmits many powerful lessons: First, it teaches that it is okay to dream, to create and believe in the achievement of visions and targets. Second, it teaches that through action research and thoughtful reflection, it is possible to design strategies that can help realize those dreams. Most important, it teaches that the die is never completely cast. We can always learn from experience and get better at whatever it is we truly care about and value.

Institutionalizing the Ethic of Action Research

The Washoe County School District is a large school system serving the city of Reno, Nevada, and its surrounding communities. For several years, the district has embraced action research as part of its strategy to foster continuous improvement and professional development.

A few years ago, the staff in the district began carrying cards in their wallets that captured the essence of what they were working to accomplish (see Figure 11.1). On one side of the card it says, *Washoe County School District—Our Goal: Continuous improvement in student performance based upon disciplined use of data.* On the reverse side it says, *What Constitutes Sound Decision Making: "The Big Five"*

1. What do you want to accomplish? (Vision, target)

2. What criteria will determine success? (Assessment criteria)

3. What do you think it will take to achieve success? (Theory of action)

4. What data will you collect? (Data to inform decisions)

5. How will you share your learning? (Community of learners)

Figure 11.1   Washoe County School Goals and Endeavors Card

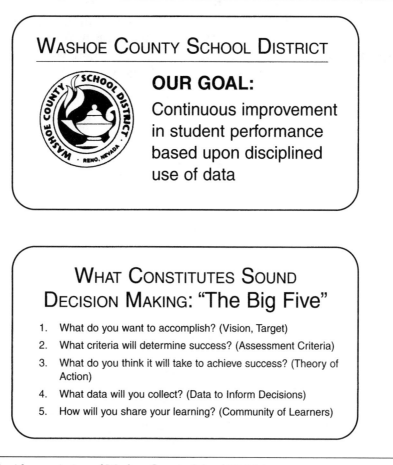

SOURCE: Used with permission of Washoe County School District.

In Washoe County, they dream of a day when The Big Five becomes a mantra chanted by everyone, to everyone, over and over, throughout the schoolhouse.

Those questions can frame discussions with students, helping them to visualize and strategize achieving their goals. They can structure discussions between classroom teachers and in doing so, reinforce the experience that colleagues are interested and excited to be working alongside one another and want to learn from each other. And finally, the Big Five forms the outline of a process for school improvement and provides a structure for ongoing discussions with parents and the community.

I truly hope that while reading this book, your participation and involvement with the four stages of action research has made you a believer in the power of the process. Chanting the Big Five mantra or finding other ways to share your belief in the empowerment that can flow from practicing the action research process can become your personal way of sharing your enthusiasm for an approach to problem solving that you have found to be professionally satisfying and have consequently made a part of your practice. When you discuss *your* vision, *your* theory, *your* data, and *your* action plans, you provide public testimony to the empowerment and satisfaction that you have received by casting yourself in the role of learner.

Building learners is more than noble work. When one believes in the innate human capacity to learn, then anything seems possible. Paraphrasing Christa

McAuliffe, when you chose teaching for your career, in no small way, you were choosing immortality. When your students learn from you how good it is to be a learner, they will have gained something that will stay with them a lifetime. Through the model you are providing, they get to see their own future: one filled with excitement, curiosity, and unlimited possibilities, and one where they, like you, can use their own learning to help others grow and develop, thereby making this a better world for us all.

Good luck and a heartfelt thank you for all that you do.

Resource A

How to Use the Feedback Forms and Summary Reports

FEEDBACK FORMS ■

- These forms were designed for use with a class in order to efficiently collect regular feedback on students' perceptions on things of interest to their teacher. Carbonless paper is used so the students can maintain a record of their responses over time.
- When using this process, it is important to think through the nature of the student perceptions you wish to collect—there are infinite possibilities. In the past, teachers have used these forms to collect data on such things as *enjoyment of the class, engagement in activities, how much students felt they learned, how difficult they found the material, how they felt during class,* and so on.
- After selecting the nature of the perceptions you want to collect, develop a rating scale for the students to use. Provide them with a copy of the scale or post it on the wall of your classroom or both. When doing this with students who aren't able to comprehend the meaning of a number scale, you might choose to build a scale with a sequence of smiling or frowning faces.
- It is often a good idea to have the students look at their previous feedback reports prior to filling out new ones. This makes it more likely that they will apply the scale consistently and it will reduce the chance that changes in ratings are influenced by temporary changes in mood.
- Encourage students to provide comments to explain their ratings since often there can be several different explanations for the same score. This enables you to know the specific justification for a student's choice of score. Also, these comments will later assist the students recalling what they were thinking when they provided the feedback.
- Be sure the students date their feedback forms. This will prove important when you and they attempt to interpret the rationale for any trends found in the ratings (e.g., the relationship between their reactions and the teaching technique being used).

■ SUMMARY REPORTS

- These carbonless forms serve two purposes. They save you, the teacher researcher, the time required to ascertain patterns of changes, as you look for trends with individual students or within particular classes. Second, they will cause your students to reflect on the changes that occurred in their perspectives over the course of the class or the term of your study, which will enable them to develop a deeper understanding of themselves as learners.

- Another value of the summary form is that it provides you with an additional and important piece of triangulated data: the students' personal explanations of the reasons behind changes that occurred in their perspectives. Later you will be able to compare and contrast their explanations with your own observations.

- When having students fill out the summary reports, use the following steps:

  1. Have the students plot their numerical ratings on the two graphs. If you are doing this with students who don't yet understand how to plot scores on a graph, have a parent volunteer or older student plot the scores for the student.

  2. Ask the students to look for changes in the direction and slope of the lines on their graphs and make tentative conclusions about the trends. For example, a student might conclude something like, "I enjoyed this project more and more as time went on," or "I got frustrated in the middle of last week."

  3. Then ask the students to sequentially review the written comments they provided on the feedback forms and reflect on the reasons for changes in perceptions. The student should then record those explanations or thoughts in the space provided below the graphs on the summary form. Should you be doing this with students who are unable to write their own responses, ask an adult or older student to pose the questions to the students and then write down their responses.

Resource B

Five Characteristics of a Quality Action Research Project

CHARACTERISTIC 1: EXPLANATION OF CONTEXT, PROBLEM, ISSUE ▪

Elements	Significance of issue for teachers and learners Unique or general factors impacting issue Potential for change or improvement

Strong	*Proficient*	*Developing*	*Basic*
Makes strong case for the need and desirability for improvement	Adequately explains the benefits for the researcher's teaching or the student's learning	Demonstrates awareness of possible benefits for teaching and learning	Declares the hope for change and improvement
Perceives and explores a broad range of implications beyond the case at hand	Recognizes and explains the applicability of this inquiry to other educators	Seems unsure or unclear about relevance beyond the case at hand	Doesn't address applicability beyond the case at hand
Provides readers with enough contextual data to take into account the uniqueness of the context	Recognizes and addresses the relevant and unique characteristics of the researcher's context	Provides accurate but incomplete report on research context	Reports on context but leaves out several critical details

■ CHARACTERISTIC 2: THEORETICAL PERSPECTIVE

Elements	Understanding or awareness of applicable literature Logic behind and reasonableness of approach Clarity of expression

Strong	*Proficient*	*Developing*	*Basic*
Provides a thorough literature review presented in a logical, clear, and concise manner	Demonstrates an understanding of key research findings or commentaries on the issue or problem	Shows a basic understanding of major premises behind intervention	Demonstrates awareness of the procedures recommended by developers of an intervention
Detailed, logical, and clear explanation for the theory informing the proposed intervention	Provides a logical and clear explanation of the researcher's theory	Explains the rationale behind proposed intervention	Explains how the researcher intends to implement the intervention
The proposed intervention logically follows from the findings of others and the researcher's own theory	The proposed intervention is justified based on the researcher's theoretical stance		

CHARACTERISTIC 3: RESEARCH DESIGN ■

Elements	Potential for yielding valid findings Potential for yielding reliable findings Consideration of extraneous or intervening variables

Strong	*Proficient*	*Developing*	*Basic*
The research design takes into account and adequately controls for most apparent and possible extraneous or intervening variables	The research design makes appropriate use of triangulation to corroborate and support findings	The research design uses authentic or recognized techniques to determine impact	A technique or techniques are proposed to demonstrate impact
The research design uses sampling techniques that make accurate findings highly likely	The research design makes use of multiple data points to increase accuracy	The research design reflects an awareness of the risk of inaccuracy	The techniques have the potential for accurately reflecting performance

■ CHARACTERISTIC 4: ANALYSIS OF DATA

Elements	Supportable and logical conclusions Alternative explanations addressed Limitations explained

Strong	*Proficient*	*Developing*	*Basic*
All reported findings and conclusions are supported by multiple and credible pieces of data	All findings are supported by credible pieces of data	The conclusions are logical and generally supported by the available data	Conclusions are not contradicted by the available data
Reasonable alternative interpretations of the data are recognized and discussed	Reasonable alternative interpretations of data are reported	The potential for alternative interpretation is recognized	
Reasonable limitations are recognized and addressed along with suggestions for overcoming them	Reasonable limitations are addressed	The researcher shows an awareness that possible limitations exist	

CHARACTERISTIC 5: ACTION PLANNING ■

Elements	Supported by findings Potential for improvement theoretically sound Contains an action research assessment design Outlines potential value for self and others

Strong	*Proficient*	*Developing*	*Basic*
The plan is a direct and logical extension of the findings and conclusions	The plan is consistent with the data and conclusions	The plan has reasonable face validity	The plan is consistent with a theory
Based on the available data, it appears likely that student performance will improve if and when the plan is followed	The findings suggest that the plan will make a difference in student performance	The available data appears supportive of the plan	The plan is not contradicted by available data
The theory behind the plan is clearly outlined and addressed	The theory behind the plan is addressed	The plan seems logical	
The assessment plan should provide valuable evidence of the effectiveness of the plan	The action plan contains a viable assessment strategy		
The researcher and other educators are likely to benefit from data on the eventual implementation of the plan	The researcher should benefit from data on the implementation of the action plan		

Glossary

This is a listing of terms used throughout this book, many of which have more than one meaning even within the field of action research. This glossary defines these words and phrases as they are used in this book.

Academic Postmortem: A comprehensive review of the educational and instructional activities that preceded and likely contributed to a particular educational outcome

Achievement Target: A performance or outcome that one believes can be influenced by the actions of educators

Adequate Yearly Progress (AYP): The rate of growth expected of a student or group of students over the course of a school year

Analytic Discourse: The process of being interviewed by a group of colleagues to assist in articulating, clarifying, and deepening one's perspective on an issue

Boundaries: Limits placed on the scope of an inquiry or activity to assist in maintaining focus

Causation: A supposition that a particular action is responsible for producing a specified result

Context: Factors found in an environment that may have an influence on what works or doesn't work in that environment

Dependent Variable: The behavior, outcome, or performance that one expects to see changed as a result of targeted action

Descriptive Research: An inquiry or study that seeks to answer the question of what is currently going on in a specified arena

Educated Hypothesis: An assumption or prediction regarding what will result from a particular action based upon past experience

Extraneous Variable: A factor that has nothing to do with the phenomenon under study (the relationships between the dependent and independent variables) and that exerts its own separate effect on the dependent variable

Face Validity: Something that seems obvious or true based on simply looking at it

Hypothesis: A prediction of what will result from an action or set of actions

Intervening Variable: A phenomenon that has its own relationship with the independent variable and has a separate influence on the dependent variable

Literature Review: A systematic examination of what has been written or reported on a phenomenon

Performance Targets: Particular skills, outcomes, or performances that one would like to see improved

Principal Investigator (PI): The person with primary leadership responsibility for a research project. This individual sets the focus, articulates the theory, and establishes the research design that guides the study

Process Targets: Professional techniques, actions, or procedures that one would like to see improved

Qualitative Data: Material that is collected or assembled pertaining to a phenomenon being studied, made up of descriptions, opinions, artifacts, or some combination of these; frequently subjective in nature

Quantitative Data: Material that is collected or assembled pertaining to the phenomenon being studied that is made up of objective ratings or scores that can be expressed mathematically

Quasi-Experimental Research: An inquiry or investigation that infers a relationship between an action or set of actions and a defined target (dependent variable)

Rate of Growth: The speed at which progress is being made on an achievement target

Rating Scale: A pre-established continuum of performance that can be used to reliably determine a level of performance on an achievement target (also referred to as a rubric)

Reflective Interview: A discourse with a colleague designed to identify and explore a potential action research focus

Relationship: A pattern of consistent influence between factors, variables, programs, or actions

Reliability: The accuracy of the data

Research Assistant (RA): An individual who assists in carrying out an investigation or study as a subordinate to the principal investigator (PI)

Researcher's Journal: Notes kept by an action researcher for the purpose of tracking events that transpire during the course of research, especially any deviations from a pre-established theory of action

Spreadsheet: An expandable record-keeping matrix (either paper or electronic) that enables a researcher to assemble data on numerous variables across a large number of subjects

Team Reflection: A process for a work group to deliberate in an effort to arrive at a collective research focus

Tentative Assertions: Statements regarding patterns or trends that surfaced during the analysis of action research data

Theory of Action: The rationale behind the actions to be taken by a practitioner and the particular inferences that back up that rationale

Trend Analysis: Looking for patterns in data over time to identify any relationships between changes in performance and specific actions and events

Universal Student Success: All students meeting academic expectations without gaps in performance due to demographic or socioeconomic factors

Validity: The truthfulness of data; whether the data does, in fact, represents what it purports to represent

Vision: The overall picture of what one would like to see accomplished as a result of action

References

Caro-Bruce, C., & Zeichner, K. (1988). The *nature and impact of an action research professional development program in one urban school district.* Madison, WI: Madison Metropolitan School District.

Deming, W. E. (2000). *Out of crisis.* Cambridge: MIT Press. (Original work published in 1986)

Depree, M. (1998). *Leading without power.* San Francisco: Jossey-Bass.

Fullan, M. (2001). *Leading in a culture of change.* San Francisco: Jossey-Bass.

Gardner, H., Csikzentmihalyi, M., & and Damon, W. (2001). *Good work: When excellence and ethics meet.* New York: Basic Books.

Hargreaves, A. (1991). Teaching and guilt: Exploring the emotions of teaching. *Teaching and Teacher Education, 7*(5/6), 491–505.

Hersey, P., & Blanchard, K. H. (1993). *Management of organizational behavior: Utilizing human resources* (6th ed.). Englewood Cliffs, NJ: Prentice Hall.

Hord, S. (1997). *Professional learning communities: Communities of continuous inquiry and improvement.* Austin, TX: Southwest Educational Development Laboratory.

Joyce, B., & Calhoun, E. (1996). *Learning experiences in school renewal: An exploration of five successful programs.* Eugene, OR: ERIC Clearinghouse on Educational Management. (ERIC Document Reproduction Services No. ED401600)

Kemmis, S., & McTaggart, R. (Eds.). (1988). *The action research planner.* Victoria, BC: Deakin University.

Little, J. W. (1982). Norms of collegiality and experimentation: Workplace conditions of school success. *American Educational Research Journal, 19,* 325–340. (ERIC Document Reproduction Services No. EJ 275 511)

Miles, M., & Huberman, A. M. (1994). *Qualitative data analysis* (2nd ed.). Thousand Oaks, CA: Sage.

No Child Left Behind Act of 2001, Pub.L. No. 107-110 (2002).

Rosenholtz, S. J. (1985). *Teachers' workplace: A study of social organization of schools.* New York: Longman.

Sagor, R. (1995, April). Overcoming the one solution syndrome. *Educational Leadership, 52*(7), 24–27.

Sagor, R. (1996). *Local control and accountability: How to get it, keep it, and improve school performance.* Thousand Oaks, CA: Corwin.

Sagor, R. (2000). *Guiding school improvement with action research.* Alexandria, VA: Association for Supervision and Curriculum Development.

Sagor, R. (2003). *Motivating students and teachers in an era of standards.* Alexandria, VA: Association for Supervision and Curriculum Development.

Sagor, R., & Curley, J. (1991, April). *Can collaborative action research improve school effectiveness?* Paper presented at AERA Annual Meeting, Chicago, IL. (ERIC Document Reproduction Services Nos. ED 336 864 & EA 023 349)

Senge, P. M. (1990). *The fifth discipline: The art and practice of the learning organization.* New York: Doubleday Currency.

Sizer, T. R. (1984). *Horace's compromise: The dilemma of the American high school.* New York: Houghton Mifflin.

Index

Page numbers in *italics* reference a figure or table.